Berlin

Berlin ist zu groß für Berlin ('Berlin Is Too Big for Berlin')
is the intriguing title of a book by the *flâneur* Hanns Zischler,
a humorous take on the sparse population of this sprawling,
polycentric city. This emptiness creates a sense of liberty and
space, but Berlin is too big for Berlin in a broader sense, too:
how can it live with and simultaneously feed the flame of
its somewhat burdensome reputation as an ultra-cool city?
Answering this question requires a trip back to the 1990s and
the origins of the myth, a period when time seemed to have
stopped: everywhere you looked you could see the scars of
war, crumbling buildings, coal-fired stoves, spartan mini-
markets. Up and down endless flights of stairs you'd walk, as so
few apartment blocks had lifts or working intercoms. Visiting
Berlin was a hallucinogenic experience, a journey into the past
and into the future at the same time. The city's youth seemed
to have assimilated completely Karl Scheffler's famous 19th-
century aphorism that Berlin is a city 'condemned for ever to
becoming and never to being', although that was seen as a good
thing. Searching for abandoned ruins, hunting for antiques at
flea markets, illegal parties in basements, all these are things
of the past. That era of urban archaeology is definitively over.
The buildings have been renovated, the squats have been cleared
and the shops furnished in typical East German style have gone.
With the healing of the scars of the past, the city's body is perhaps
less dramatic, but it is certainly stronger and in ruder health.
Berliners, too, have lost something of that sense of heartache
– that romantic, self-destructive streak – and today some
people even come to Berlin to work and not to 'create' or simply
do nothing. But Berlin is still a youthful city with no morbid
attachment to its 'poor-but-sexy' past, committed instead
to holding on to what it holds most dear: its uncompromising
multiculturalism and the certainty that the future is yet to be
written. To quote someone who knows the city well, Berlin
is and always will be 'pure potential'.

Contents

The photographs in this issue were taken by the photojournalist and documentary photographer **Mattia Vacca**, a long-time contributor to *Corriere della Sera*. Inspired by his interest in social issues and the consequences of armed conflicts in different parts of the world, in 2018 he published the photography book *Confine*, the collective story of how the city of Como, on the border between Switzerland and Italy, came to be the site of a refugee camp. He joined the photographic agency Prospekt in 2018. His work has featured in titles such as *The New Republic*, the *Guardian*, the *Daily Telegraph*, the *Independent*, *Wired*, *Esquire*, *L'Espresso*, *Süddeutsche Zeitung Magazin* and *Público*, earning him numerous awards, including the Sony World Photography Award, the Royal Photographic Society Award, the UNESCO Humanity Photo Award and the New York Photo Award.

Berlin in Numbers

POPULATION DENSITY

Density per km².

Paris	///////////////////////	20,909
Athens	//////////////////////	19,135
Brussels	//////////	7,282
Lisbon	/////////	6,446
Amsterdam	//////	5,135
Berlin	■■■	**4,162**
Rome	/////	3,389

SOURCE: BERLIN-BRANDENBURG OFFICE OF STATISTICS

GETTING AROUND THE CITY

Mobility in European capitals.

☐ Car ▨ Public transport
■ Bicycle ▨ On foot

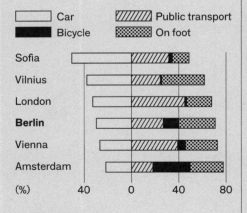

Sofia
Vilnius
London
Berlin
Vienna
Amsterdam

(%) 40 0 40 80

SOURCE: EPOMM / DIVV

FAR FROM THE CROWD

Berlin population change (after 1920 other communities were incorporated into the city).

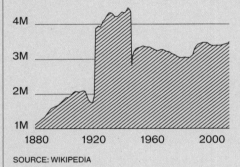

4M
3M
2M
1M
1880 1920 1960 2000

SOURCE: WIKIPEDIA

STREET LAMP STYLES

Of the 224,000 street lamps in Berlin, 30,000 are lit by gas. There are four different models:

26,000   280   2,800   920

SOURCE: BERLIN.DE

SALARIES

Net monthly income for people in work.

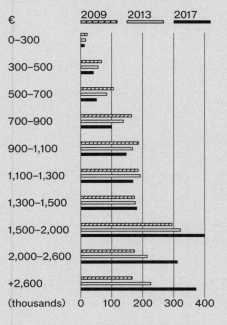

€ — 2009 / 2013 / 2017

€	
0–300	
300–500	
500–700	
700–900	
900–1,100	
1,100–1,300	
1,300–1,500	
1,500–2,000	
2,000–2,600	
+2,600	

(thousands) 0   100   200   300   400

SOURCE: AMT FÜR STATISTIK BERLIN-BRANDENBURG

POOR ...

Per capita GDP in Germany (2018).

1
Wolfsburg
€182,301

11
Munich
€79,690

21
Hamburg
€64,771

25
Cologne
€59,588

74
Berlin
€40,105

SOURCE: WIKIPEDIA

... BUT SEXY

3M

Number of people coming to Berlin to dance, bringing in €1.48 million (2019).

SEARCH: MORGENPOST

DÖNER VS. CURRYWURST

70M

Currywurst a year

146M

Döner a year

SOURCE: VISITBERLIN.DE

INNOVATION

Frankfurt is Germany's financial hub, but Berlin has become Europe's centre for fintech.

1 **Berlin**
2 Paris
3 Amsterdam
4 Dublin
5 Vilnius
6 Moscow
7 Madrid
8 Barcelona

SOURCE: GLOBAL
FINTECH INDEX, 2020

ICH BIN KEIN BERLINER

20% of the population of Berlin was born outside Germany.

Where the non-native Berliners come from (thousands)

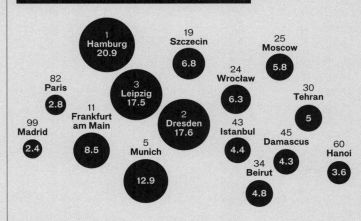

- 1 Hamburg 20.9
- 19 Szczecin 6.8
- 25 Moscow 5.8
- 82 Paris 2.8
- 3 Leipzig 17.5
- 24 Wrocław 6.3
- 30 Tehran 5
- 99 Madrid 2.4
- 11 Frankfurt am Main 8.5
- 2 Dresden 17.6
- 43 Istanbul 4.4
- 45 Damascus 4.3
- 60 Hanoi 3.6
- 5 Munich 12.9
- 34 Beirut 4.8

SOURCE: BERLIN-BRANDENBURG [...] / INTERAKTIV.MORGENPOST

A Sign of the Times

ANDREA D'ADDIO
Translated by Alan Thawley

Berlin, 1999. Manni has absent-mindedly left a bag full of money on the U-Bahn. If he doesn't get it back in the next twenty minutes he will be bumped off by a local criminal. From one of the distinctive yellow phone boxes, he phones his girlfriend Lola to ask for help. Lola agrees. She has three possible courses of action: asking her father for money, stealing it or gambling at the casino. There is one constant in all these options: she must act fast. She has no car, so Lola starts to run, taking her past some of Berlin's iconic landmarks: the Oberbaumbrücke, the red bridge that was once a border crossing between East and West, the legendary Friedrichstrasse, the Gendarmenmarkt with its twin churches and Museum Island. Providing the backdrop for this story with three endings is a city of construction sites, run-down buildings, old socialist signs for abandoned shops and street art on every corner. Twenty years on, and that Berlin no longer exists, nor would it be possible to tell the story of Tom Tykwer's wonderful film *Run, Lola, Run* (*Lola rennt*) today. The city has been invaded by electric scooters and bikes for rent via smartphone apps, the U-Bahns

are continually monitored by CCTV, and on a walk through the centre you'll see all the buildings have been renovated and now command rents similar to those in London.

Back then, ten years after the Wall had come down, the city was going through its rebellious phase, when anything, or almost anything, was permitted. Residential buildings, factories and former warehouses on the socialist side were up for grabs by whoever wanted to move in or set up a studio. East Berliners had fled to the West, not just West Berlin but also West Germany. The local authorities rented out the properties that no one wanted to live in for a handful of Deutschmarks a month in the hope of attracting young people, pushing up their value and then taking them back to sell on to property speculators (see 'The Evicted Generation' on page 137). The strategy worked. The central Mitte district (*Mitte* means 'centre' in German) was home to the legendary Tacheles arts centre, providing accommodation and studio space for artists from all over Europe. All around was a string of old basements transformed into bars where you could go and dance. Often lacking an official name, these places were named

after the day of the week when they would regularly host the city's most popular party. Since work was hard to come by and poorly paid, any day of the week could be the right one to stay up until dawn, so Dienstag (Tuesday) could well be busier than Freitag (Friday). Being able to speak German was essential: half of the population had learned Russian as their second language at school, while the other half associated the English language with the USA, which had maintained a military presence in the city for over forty years, waiting for the Cold War to lose its adjective.

Today, walking through any area inside the Ring, an orbital route around the city centre consisting of two elevated S-Bahn lines, you are as likely to hear people speaking Italian, French, Spanish or English as you are to meet a genuine Berliner. Turks are still the largest non-German community in the city, followed by the Poles. Whereas once people moved to Berlin to feel part of an anti-establishment community, nowadays people come to take advantage of professional opportunities that are all but unthinkable elsewhere. The seeds of creativity that fell almost by chance on the fallow ground of a city that people imagined would always remain 'poor but sexy' (as it was described by former mayor Klaus Wowereit), ended up attracting investors in search of an unconventional environment to grow their start-ups. The fruits of that period of the city's history are now on-trend European companies such as Zalando, N26, Soundcloud and Omio. Brexit, with its drain of capital and people, is contributing to the dizzying rise in the cost of living in Berlin. The old residents have been pushed to the margins of the city, whereas it only takes a few years for all the newcomers to feel entitled, rightly or wrongly, to jokingly quote Kennedy's now famous 1963 phrase 'Ich bin ein Berliner' ('I am a Berliner'). In this sense, in its ability to welcome people and ensure that their residential address dovetails with a characteristic of their personality, Berlin – fortunately – has yet to change. And perhaps it never will.

Dress Code

FALKO HENNIG
Translated by Stephen Smithson

Visitors to Berlin are often surprised at first to see so many homeless people on the streets – until it dawns on them that what they're seeing is just Berliners dressed in their regular clothes. In their turn, once these visitors leave the city their everyday clothes are transformed into rags. Dress codes – Berliners use the English term but write it as a single word, 'dresscodes' – are different here from the rest of Germany; Berlin is distinguished by higher levels of tolerance, but because the rules are less sharply defined it can be difficult to adhere to them. A good example is the Berghain techno club, which officially has no dress code. Look for a recipe for guaranteed admission to the club and all you'll find are details of what will guarantee that you get turned away. It's said that the wrong outfit will cause the dreaded bouncer-in-chief Sven Marquardt to refuse entry, and attempting to discuss the matter with the comprehensively tattooed and pierced ex-punk from East Germany is not advised. There is no dress code, just rumours; KiK or H&M are not recommended, it's said, but then getting in is no problem if you're dressed in black, in leather or in nothing at all.

Personally, I'm an adherent of naturism – what the Germans call FKK, or *Freikörperkultur* – and find it a great shame that this fashion is for the most part followed only by people who are in their eighties and above. The naturist movement started in Berlin in the late 19th century, and is still thriving in the Tiergarten, the Grunewald forest and at the Plötzensee lake – and at *Schlagernacktparty* events, which involve dancing naked to retro-pop.

The nudists' founding principle is that the human body is not ugly but beautiful and one should not be ashamed of it. Covering the sex organs, of all things, only to draw attention to them with brightly coloured clothing – this is something that naturists find particularly tasteless and obscene. But it's the elderly practitioners of naturism – with their lack of muscle tone and the slackness of their skin, with their age spots, surgical scars and varicose veins – who put the ideal of beauty into perspective.

'Berlin Originals' have been around for a long time, and their 'originality' lies not just in their behaviour but in the way they dress. Past examples include the Hauptmann von Köpenick (real name,

Wilhelm Voigt), a poor man who donned a captain's uniform and masqueraded as a Prussian military officer, and Gertrud Müller, who played the barrel organ while dressed as a chimney sweep. Her act was immortalised on her gravestone, on which she is remembered not only as a chimney sweep/barrel-organ player but also, by virtue of the occupation denoted by her last name, as a mill girl; the result is *Schornsteinfegerleierkastenmüllerin* – a word that, even in German with its penchant for agglutinative 'tapeworm' compounds, stands out for its length. Another original was Strohhut-Emil – Straw-Hat Emil – who, by using a hidden mechanism, was able to flip open the top of his headwear.

Current Berlin Originals tend to gather in the tourist area between the TV tower and the Brandenburg Gate, where you will come across, for example, an organ grinder in a Prussian uniform and spiked helmet or a man in 1920s clothing, his face tattooed Maori style, accompanied by a huge parrot. You may also see someone walking around as Frederick the Great – complete with wig, cane and sword.

For decades one man, the Schallplatte ('vinyl record') – whose most noticeable attribute is the long-playing record in his hair – has been a fixture in the area around Rosenthaler Platz. 'Where we come from he would be locked up,' a guide was told by a group of tourists. 'That's precisely why he's in Berlin,' the guide responded, unfazed.

It is rare to see people out barefoot in Berlin. A few years ago my daughter and her boyfriend took to walking around the city without shoes, and we parents relaxed only when, after suffering a number of injuries from broken glass and sharp stones, they reverted to wearing shoes. And, speaking of shoes, one of the more curious fashions to experience a spike in popularity in recent times is the toe shoe; these look a bit like gloves except that they are made of rubber. I find the idea of shops that sell these as absurd as the concept of a nudist clothing store, which only exemplifies my bourgeois pettiness. I certainly don't walk around barefoot, but I do wear a nice pair of sandals. Only after I've been playing football, when I happily take off my sweaty shoes, shin-pads and socks, do I go around in bare feet – but on my bike.

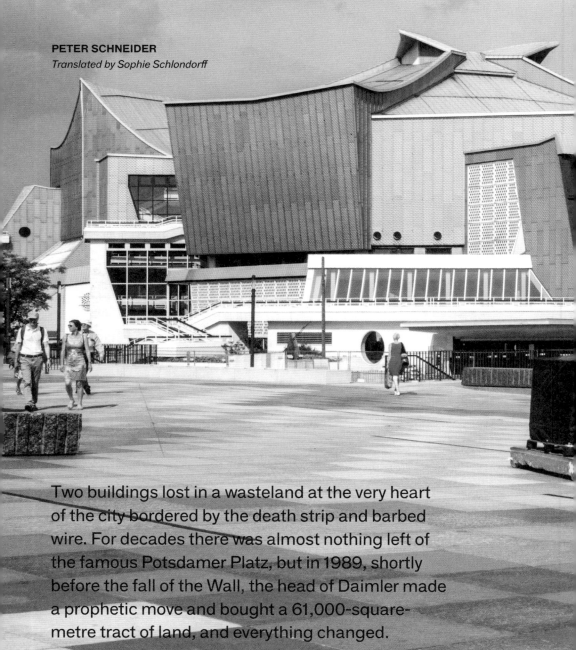

The Greatest Show in Town:

PETER SCHNEIDER
Translated by Sophie Schlondorff

Two buildings lost in a wasteland at the very heart of the city bordered by the death strip and barbed wire. For decades there was almost nothing left of the famous Potsdamer Platz, but in 1989, shortly before the fall of the Wall, the head of Daimler made a prophetic move and bought a 61,000-square-metre tract of land, and everything changed.

The Resurrection of Potsdamer Platz

The Berliner Philharmonie concert hall
with Potsdamer Platz in the background.

13

The most contested construction site was Potsdamer Platz.

This square, which had been the busiest intersection in Europe in the 1920s, had turned into Berlin's biggest urban wasteland during the Cold War. Any building that had managed to survive the bombing of the Second World War reasonably intact had subsequently been torn down. On 13 August 1961, along the line that had been painted on the asphalt to mark the border between the three western sectors and the Soviet sector since August 1948, the Wall went up. Under the pretext of needing to protect the western border against the alleged daily threat of invasion by 'imperialist forces', East German authorities tore down almost all of the remaining buildings located within their territory. As a result, Potsdamer Platz had become a building cemetery of sorts, without tombstones. Only older Berliners could still conjure up the ghosts of these former buildings in their minds' eyes.

Until the early 1990s the square was dominated by the one structure that had replaced the vanished buildings: the Berlin Wall. On the western side of the almost 500-yard-wide (500-metre) desert at the centre of the city, a platform surrounded by snack bars and souvenir stands had been put up, from which curious bystanders could observe the Wall. There they stood, looking directly into the binoculars of the border police at their guard posts, who, in turn, stared straight back into the tourists' own.

Only one building had survived the demolition mania: Weinhaus Huth, a wine house built in the early 20th century by the wine-dealer Willy Huth on a lot purchased by his grandfather. To support the load of his wine stock, Willy Huth had had it built with a steel-frame construction, a technique that was new at the time. Thanks to this provision, as well as to sheer luck, the building had survived the bombing and artillery fire of the Second World War with minimal damage. For decades the Weinhaus – together with the remains of the bombed-out Hotel Esplanade – sat like a prehistoric boulder on the otherwise desolate Potsdamer Platz.

Whenever I drove from Charlottenburg towards Kreuzberg and saw the building standing there, I'd inevitably shake my head in disbelief. The image could have been from a Western shot in Arizona: a lone building in the middle of a desert, rising up like a mirage before the eyes of a thirsty cowboy after a long ride – and its name, at least, delivered what it seemed to promise: a good drink. Except that this particular forsaken building happened to be located at the centre of a major city. It was a fixed star in a barren wasteland, a preposterous beacon. Who lived behind those glowing windows, who held down the fort in this far-flung outpost in the former city centre to the west of the Wall, the construction

PETER SCHNEIDER was born in Lübeck, Germany, and has lived in Berlin on and off since the 1960s. Political commitment is at the heart of his early work, and in the late 1960s he was a key spokesperson for the West German radical student movement. German current affairs, the fall of the Wall and the reunification of Germany later became important themes in his work, notably in *The Wall Jumper* (Penguin, 2005) and *Berlin Now: The Rise of the City and the Fall of the Wall* (Farrar, Straus and Giroux USA / Penguin UK, 2014), from which this article is taken. He has taught at several universities – including Stanford, Princeton and Harvard – and written for many international newspapers including *Der Spiegel*, *The New York Times*, *Le Monde* and *La Repubblica*.

> '*Potsdamer Platz became the preferred location of politicians and presidents from around the world for visiting and making public appearances.*'

of which had relegated the building to the edge of the world?

Books and articles about the Weinhaus tell us that Willy Huth continued to run a pub there for a long time after the Wall went up. He couldn't bring himself to sell the family legacy, although by now its iron girders were rusted and its wine-storage spaces filled with rubble. Occasionally he could also be seen on the roof of the building, looking out over the empty square where [one of] the world's first traffic lights had once controlled the flow of traffic.

Willy Huth died shortly after his ninetieth birthday party. The West Berlin authorities were at a loss as to what to do with the building. In 1967 Willy Huth's widow had sold it and the attached property to the West Berlin Tiergarten district for a pittance. The bureaucrats of the Social Democratic Party decided to use the building as public housing. But instead of the families with multiple children they had anticipated, it was mostly loners, masters of the art of living, painters and castaways, with their preference for unorthodox living arrangements, who moved in. And, after all, what was a family supposed to do with an apartment located in the middle of an enormous, undeveloped plot divided by a wall? There were no bakeries nearby, let alone supermarkets; no schools, no kindergartens; the closest bus stop was a ten-minute walk away. The U-Bahn trains thundering underground through the sealed-off Potsdamer Platz ghost station every few minutes made an earth-shattering noise.

The tenants who lived in the building in the 1980s were treated to novel sights and sounds several times a year. Potsdamer Platz became the preferred location of politicians and presidents from around the world for visiting and making public appearances. Watching from their balconies or through open windows, the tenants of Weinhaus Huth enjoyed the best seats in the house.

The writer Inka Bach had grown up in East Berlin and fled from East Germany with her family in 1972. In the summer of 1989, after several extended stays in New York and Paris, she moved into Haus Huth with her newborn son. And so the girl from East Germany unexpectedly found herself at the juncture of East and West Berlin.

An 800-square-foot (240-square-metre) loft with a small bedroom, it was hardly ideal for a young family, which soon grew to include Inka's second child, a daughter. While there was a huge amount of space outside for playing, there were few other children. Getting to the supermarket or bus stop was inconvenient. Sure, Inka was living in the old heart of the former capital and had what seemed at the time to be an 'unobstructable view'. But there were unique advantages as well. Inka never had any trouble finding a parking spot for her minivan directly in front of the building, and the police didn't give out tickets anywhere in the greater vicinity of Weinhaus Huth. At 2.50 Deutschmarks ($1.30) per square metre, the rent was a dream. And while she may have needed a car to pick up day-to-day essentials, the Berlin Philharmonic, Martin-Gropius-Bau and New National Gallery were all within walking distance.

THE POLISH MARKET

Between late 1988 and 1989, Polish traders descended on West Berlin en masse at weekends, taking advantage of the freedom to travel conceded by the communist government in 1988. Like all the Soviet bloc countries, Poland was suffering an economic crisis that grew even worse over the following years, so many people headed to West Berlin to sell their wares. Rather than professional traders, however, they were often ordinary citizens, including many seniors, who set up their stalls to bring in a little extra money and help make ends meet. The vast, empty space of Potsdamer Platz was the ideal location for this flea market reminiscent of a bazaar, where the Poles came to sell goods of all kinds: animals in cages, cheeses, sausages and, above all, alcohol and cigarettes, all laid out on a simple sheet on the ground. The bargain prices attracted hordes of visitors, and the illegal market grew week by week during 1989, ultimately attracting public criticism. People demanded its closure because of the mess, chaos and supposed illicit activities, including prostitution, which spread throughout the surrounding area. However, many Berliners benefited from the hustle and bustle, as it was not uncommon for the Poles to spend the wads of cash they scraped together on consumer electronics right there in West Berlin. The Polish market was closed down and banned several times but continued to switch locations and cause controversy until it was eclipsed by the events of autumn 1989. Today Berlin is home to more than a hundred thousand people of Polish origin, the second largest non-German community after the Turks.

The building's other occupants weren't exactly the sort of tenants the Tiergarten district office had hoped for. The renter next door, a gay dermatologist from Munich, had a weakness for old Berlin brass doorknobs. At some point he was found dead in his apartment, having shot himself. His apartment was overflowing with Nazi emblems and relics – a collection that apparently had little or nothing to do with the mentally disturbed man's convictions. An actress from East Germany, who was trying her hand at the esoteric arts after abandoning a career in theatre, lived on the fifth floor – supposedly she was a close friend of the East German dissident and civil rights activist Bärbel Bohley. Far-Eastern scents and meditation music wafted into the stairwell from her apartment. Sometimes Inka would get a massage from this neighbour. The woman's name later showed up on a list of informers for East Germany's state security service. From that point on Inka stopped availing herself of the mystic's services. She would baffle her friends by telling them that she had been 'in the hands of the Stasi' twice a week.

Another long-time tenant of Haus Huth had planted a garden on the overgrown street in front of the building. The garden took up a section of Potsdamer Strasse that no one had driven on for decades but that had once been a main artery of the traffic hub of Berlin. She never imagined that her little garden had become the focus of a global corporation that wanted to build on this very spot.

But the idyllic state of affairs on the Potsdamer Platz wasteland changed – even before the fall of the Wall. The rabbits that had been moving freely back and forth between East and West for years were now joined by new border crossers: in the summer of 1989 Poles started showing up by the Landwehr Canal and near Potsdamer Platz on weekends, bringing souvenirs with them: tools, chinaware, a painting on wood of the Madonna with child. West Berliners, used to dealing with Turkish salespeople, discovered that it's impossible to haggle with Poles. It remained a mystery how these inexperienced vendors from the neighbouring eastern state managed to get into West Berlin. Arriving Saturday morning, they were gone again by Sunday night.

Then the Wall came down. For months Inka heard the hammering of the 'Wall woodpeckers' hacking away at the monstrosity day and night. After the rabbits and the Poles, the 'city Indians' arrived with their tents and corrals of wagons, laying siege to Potsdamer Platz. It was Inka's son who alerted her to the new possibilities after the fall of the Wall. Inka had always taken her children with her on her daily walks to the Gropius-Bau and the New National Gallery, which the city's culture buffs could reach only by bus or taxi. Where other kids demanded the 'playground', for Inka's children the word was 'Gropius-Bau'. At one point her son, an enthusiastic walker, discovered a kindergarten on the eastern side of the Wall. Inka valiantly enrolled him in the kindergarten, which was still being run by a staff from the state she had fled. It was clear to her that her spectacular view from the third floor would not remain 'unobstructable'. Her family's days in Haus Huth were numbered.

Shortly before the fall of the Wall, Edzard Reuter, the CEO of the Daimler Group at the time, bought fifteen thousand acres (61,000 square metres) to the southwest of Potsdamer Platz from the West Berlin Senate. The sale, which was made at a time when hardly anyone believed in an imminent end to the divided state of Germany let alone in the dissolution of the Soviet Union, was a bold – a prophetic

Above: In the 1930s Potsdamer Platz was one of Europe's busiest intersections. In the centre of the square were the city's first traffic lights, installed in 1924, and behind it Erich Mendelsohn's ultra-modern Columbushaus, which survived the war but was demolished in 1957.

Below: 1972, and Potsdamer Platz and Leipziger Platz have been turned into a no man's land.

Above: Haus Huth in its splendid isolation.
(© Ullstein Bild, Getty Images)

Below: Remnants of the Wall and the Infobox, a temporary building that stood from 1995 to 2001; it was used as an exhibition space and information centre for the building works.
(© Ullstein Bild, Getty Images)

'All that was missing was an appearance by the Berlin band Einstürzende Neubauten, which, presumably because of its name – "collapsing new buildings" – was never invited.'

– investment. Indeed, it was driven more by a political vision than by commercial interests. Edzard Reuter, who was the son of West Berlin's legendary first mayor, Ernst Reuter, wanted to build not only a new Daimler headquarters here but a whole new urban area, which would – at some distant point in the future – be connected to East Berlin. Reuter himself was surprised by how quickly his bet paid off. The plot of land, which he bought for ninety-three million Deutschmarks ($47 million), is now one of the most valuable properties in Berlin.

As an unwelcome 'dowry', Reuter had also inherited Weinhaus Huth, which the city had just spent three million Deutschmarks ($1.5 million) renovating. The building stood in the way of every possible overall design for the area but happened to be part of it. Moreover, in November 1979 the Tiergarten district office designated Weinhaus Huth a landmark, 'one of the last examples of modern commercial architecture from the Kaiser era'. Yet neither Edzard Reuter nor his architect, Renzo Piano, whose design had won the competition for the Daimler property, suspected at the time just how many headaches the building would cause them.

For the new owner-builders, Haus Huth's landmark status meant one thing above all: enormous costs and the task of integrating into their plans a relatively unexceptional turn-of-the-century Berlin commercial building, which wasn't exactly on a par with the Colosseum or Hadrian's Villa outside of Rome. The building stood on marshy ground and needed to

be underpinned, to use the construction term. Because the architects feared that a 130-foot-deep (forty-metre) construction pit being dug nearby might cause the building to sink or even collapse, they decided to place 'the gem' on a framework of pilings anchored sixty feet (eighteen metres) into the ground. There was something touching about this fifty-million-euro measure: here was the owner-builder Daimler making an effort that the Italians won't even make to safeguard the ruins of Pompeii in order to preserve a wine merchant's building with nothing exceptional about it beyond the fact that it had survived the Second World War and all the demolition that followed. The tenants, including Inka Bach, who had held down the fort in Haus Huth until the last possible moment, were given generous financial settlements to move out.

From the moment construction began, however, Daimler faced strong headwinds from both East and West. Doomsday prophets, of whom there has never been a shortage in Berlin, predicted that the construction lake would deprive the surrounding areas of groundwater; the trees in the neighbouring Tierpark would die of thirst. From the start the Daimler project was 'the most hated construction project in Berlin', reports Manfred Gentz, whom Daimler had put in charge of it. Daimler was categorically rejected as an owner-builder at Potsdamer Platz not just by the media-savvy guild of architects in East and West Berlin but also by the population of East Berlin, bolstered by a swelling chorus from the city's West. How,

THE PASSENGER   Peter Schneider

they asked, can we allow an entire area of the city to be developed by an automotive group from Stuttgart, which might well decide to lock the gates to 'its section of the city' at night? And what's the rush anyway? Why does the area have to be developed in just four years? Why not let the city grow there organically over the next twenty to thirty years? And does the entire plot really have to be covered with buildings? Couldn't part of it be set aside for the generations to come?

Manfred Gentz made up his mind to turn 'the most hated construction project in Berlin into its most popular' by opening it to the public. The idea was to involve the famously curious Berliners in the project by turning them into a permanent audience for the 'tower-building' performance. Haus Huth, Gentz decided, was a fitting location for this kind of dialogue.

From that point on Gentz regularly invited the press and West Berlin glitterati to the new operational headquarters. Weather permitting, guests would stand around on the roof of Haus Huth – glass of champagne in one hand, crab appetiser in the other – listening to the architects explain the construction in progress, peering every now and then over the edge at the brown construction-pit lake below with a slight shudder. Eventually tricks from the magic box of event culture were added to further sweeten the deal. Rock climbers were hired to rappel down the walls of the unfinished high-rises; poets from around the world recited their texts in the middle of the incomplete structures; bands performed on the most improbable makeshift stages. Truth be told, all that was missing was an appearance by the Berlin experimental punk band Einstürzende Neubauten, which, presumably because of its name – literally, 'collapsing new buildings' – was never invited.

Gentz's strategy paid off. Month after month the show site cast its spell over an ever-larger number of Berliners. On several occasions I was among the guests invited to the roof of Haus Huth. Attending one of these Daimler press conferences meant being witness to a strange spectacle at the entrance before you even got in. Cheerful and festively dressed guests searched in vain for an opening in the chain-link fence surrounding the area. Ladies in high heels and evening gowns asked for directions from construction workers, who had to take off their hard hats to hear them. Nodding in thanks, the guests headed off in the direction indicated, lifting their expensive coats and dresses, but unable to prevent their steps across the building boards from splattering mud, which flecked the ladies' white calves and their escorts' dress pants. But there was almost always a stiff wind blowing – the barely 130-foot-tall (forty-metre) building was the tallest point far and wide – so most guests were busy pulling up their coat collars and clutching their expensive hats to their heads. Once, a gust of wind snatched up an elegant lady's straw hat. She was too late in grabbing its brim, and the updraft whirled it about in a spectacular dance before it finally sailed towards the muddy groundwater-lake below.

At one of these rooftop press conferences I met Renzo Piano, the world-famous Italian architect. Since I speak Italian, we quickly struck up a conversation – a conversation that continues to this day. I studied Piano's designs, he read my books about Berlin – in the hopes of discovering something about the city's soul through them. Before coming to Berlin he would usually give me a ring.

I asked Piano whether *intelligenza leggera* ('light intelligence') could hold its own even in the northern light of the

Prussian capital – under the influence of grey sandstone and red brick. Piano admitted he was nervous about the project at Potsdamer Platz. It wasn't the usual *horror vacui*, or aversion to empty spaces, that set in before every large construction project. And it wasn't even the scope of the undertaking that he was worried about. He remembered how he felt the first time he had stepped on to the wasteland in the heart of the city – a place, as he put it, 'saturated with history. You can sense the ghosts of the past at every turn, but ghosts are all that you encounter – there's nothing you can see or touch.'

Initially, he was stumped by the task of creating urban life from this *tabula rasa*. Except for Haus Huth and the remains of the Hotel Esplanade, there were no reference points – no ensemble that might have provided inspiration or acted as a springboard. He would have liked to be able to integrate at least a section of the Wall into his designs, but the Wall had also disappeared without a trace. Wasn't this hasty disposal just another bout of the very same cleaning-up mania that had compelled German post-war planners to erase all structural traces of the pre-war era?

He didn't believe in the advantages of a *tabula rasa*, Piano said. 'A city is a text with many pages, and every page counts. Too many pages are missing from Berlin's urban history.' He had begun his work at Potsdamer Platz with the vision of a piazza with water flowing around it, the city's streets radiating outwards in a star-like formation. 'You always start with emptiness, not fullness. It's the voids in a city that determine its structure.'

At the same time, a few icons had served as points of reference for his designs, because they offered context either as existing solitary structures or even as mere ghosts of buildings. The theatre he built pays homage to Hans Scharoun's State Library, across from which it stands. The entrance tower to 'his section of the city', the Debis office high-rise, is meant to evoke a Mies van der Rohe skyscraper that was never built. Piano was inspired by the desire – technically all but impossible at the time – to counteract gravity. As executed, his designs resulted in a barely 330-foot-tall (100-metre) glass-and-steel battleaxe hurled into the sands of Brandenburg. Piano likes the fact that the facing tower, designed by Hans Kollhoff, is at odds with his own building in every way. As a counterpoint to Piano's tossed axe, Kollhoff built a classic high-rise, thoroughly elegant in its own way, out of dark-red, burned-looking brick reminiscent of New York buildings from the 1920s. Glass and steel vs. stone – why not play them off against each other?

What worried him was the incredible speed at which new urban entities arise. This material revolution, Piano said, virtually precluded the biological growth of cities. 'This is the first time in history that you can produce an entire urban area in five to ten years. It's like giving birth to a baby two months after it was conceived. You have no idea who is going to breathe life into the new neighbourhood. It has to work right away. So you take advantage of tried-and-true attractions that generate some semblance of hustle and bustle: a shopping mall, cinema, casino, theatre, public square, fountains. You create a space not for life with its unpredictable, biological rhythms, but for virtual life. This kind of awakening by bombardment scares me sometimes.'

Can't something be left unfinished, I asked, some small part of the construction area set aside for the ideas and revisions of future generations?

The financial constraints of a large-scale project like this are despotic, Piano

Above: The façade of the old Anhalter Bahnhof; the rest of the station was demolished in 1960.

THE PASSENGER   Peter Schneider

> 'It was a crazy time, an incredible time. Every few months the reawakened city would surprise its residents and visitors with yet another new, unheard-of construction "happening".'

replied. They don't allow for leaving openings. It would be expecting too much of him as an architect to leave untouched any part of an area he had been hired to develop.

The Daimler project at Potsdamer Platz was one of the very few major projects in Berlin that was completed exactly on time and on budget. The first of several big celebrations took place at the end of October 1996 to mark the topping out of a twenty-two-storey high-rise. Manfred Gentz and his colleagues had come up with something special for the occasion. Their plan was for Daniel Barenboim, the musical director of the Berlin State Opera, to conduct an unusual ballet: nineteen construction cranes would move their massive steel arms in rhythm to Beethoven's 'Ode to Joy' as conducted by the maestro. No one in Gentz's team really believed that the world-famous conductor would agree to it. But, to everyone's surprise, he did.

The night before the 'premiere', Manfred Gentz tells me, he stopped by the construction site one last time. He was puzzled to find that it was brightly lit. All of the cranes had their lights on and were going through motions that made no sense in the context of normal construction-site operations. Unrelated to any sensible task, their arms moved about in the night, like gigantic insects practising how to fly. It was some time before Gentz grasped what this

nocturnal spectacle was about. Apparently the crane operators had arranged to meet for a final dress rehearsal, possibly to the accompaniment of portable radios they had brought along.

The next day Daniel Barenboim conducted the 'Ode to Joy' from Beethoven's Ninth Symphony. Waving his left hand in the direction of the first and second violinists – the nearby cranes – then his right towards the steel monsters farther away – the horns and percussionists – he called everyone up for the tutti. The crane operators did their best to follow the conductor's vigorous gestures, which they could barely make out from the enormous height of their operating cabins.

It was a crazy time, an incredible time. Every few months the reawakened city would surprise its residents and visitors with yet another new, unheard-of construction 'happening'. Shortly before the concert of the cranes, on the other side of Potsdamer Platz, dominated by the Sony Center, the so-called Kaisersaal had been relocated.

The Kaisersaal was more or less all that was left of the legendary Hotel Esplanade after the Second World War. The neo-baroque-style hall owed its name to the last German kaiser, Wilhelm II, who had used it to host his 'gentlemen's evenings'. Greta Garbo and Charlie Chaplin, ridiculed as a 'Jewish clown' by the National Socialist newspaper *Völkischer Beobachter*, stayed at the Esplanade. In this same hotel, in 1944, conspirators in the July plot against Hitler waited for the code word 'Valkyrie'.

Following an air raid, out of the Hotel

Left: Potsdamer Platz and the Beisheim Center, built on the former Lenné Triangle.

Esplanade's total of four hundred rooms and 240 bathrooms only the Kaisersaal, imperial toilets and reading room survived intact. Until the end of the 1980s, sheep grazed behind the hotel ruins. During the years of the Wall, the Kaisersaal alone succeeded in carving out some semblance of an afterlife for itself – as an event venue and film set. Scenes for movies including *Cabaret*, *Breakthrough*, *Wings of Desire* and *Marianne and Juliane* were filmed here. The Kaisersaal never would have survived the construction work at Potsdamer Platz had it not been designated a landmark after the opening of the Wall. Just like Weinhaus Huth, it suddenly seemed indispensable – due simply to the fact that it had remained standing. These retroactively ennobled Berlin monuments are hardly going to inspire anyone to fall to his or her knees in devotion. Even so, the landmark preservationists deserve a word of thanks. Because that's just how it is in Berlin: after the destruction of the war and the architectural crimes committed afterwards, you had to learn to appreciate the chance survival of even the merely average and banal.

Originally, the architects of the Sony Center had wanted to tear down the Kaisersaal. When they drew up their plans they simply overlooked the protected landmark. Now, they unexpectedly found themselves faced with the task of integrating the bulky isolated island into their designs. The oversight apparently ended up costing the group a total of seventy-five million Deutschmarks ($50 million). The Kaisersaal couldn't just stay where it was since it stood directly in the way of the new Potsdamer Strasse, so the decision was made to relocate it. The unusual undertaking required the development of special technology. The plan was to raise the colossus some eight feet (2.5 metres) and place it on an air cushion of sorts with

THE UNEXPECTED ESCAPE

Not everyone knows that the Wall did not always faithfully track the border; in some places there might be a couple of square metres in the West that were actually part of the GDR. Others, however, were more expansive, and one of these was found in the wasteland to the north of Potsdamer Platz, the so-called Lenné Triangle, a 40,000-square-metre plot between Lennéstrasse, Bellevuestrasse (behind the Sony Center, where the Ritz Carlton hotel now stands) and Ebertstrasse. After years of talks the two sides of the city had reached an agreement that the land be transferred to West Berlin on 1 July 1988; in the meantime, though, the area, which had remained untouched for almost thirty years, had been occupied by environmentalists and left-wing activists opposing the construction of a new ring road that was due to pass right through it. Their encampment had grown into a bizarre village with a few wooden huts, goats and chickens. The police on the western side had fenced off the whole Triangle, but until the transfer came into force they did not dare intervene. Then, punctually, on 1 July nine hundred West Berlin police officers arrived in riot gear to break up the camp, but when the go-ahead was given they could not believe their eyes: 182 activists scaled the Wall using makeshift wooden ladders and fled across the death strip to the East, having made arrangements with the GDR authorities to stage the largest mass escape in the history of the Wall – but in the unexpected direction: from West to East.

the help of hydraulic levers. It would then be shifted a few feet south, where it would take a sharp turn right before floating 250 feet (seventy-five metres) west. A viewing platform was set up to allow curious onlookers to watch.

The film director Wim Wenders gave the signal for the operation to start. After this grandiose spectacle, however, it turned out that the operation to relocate the Kaisersaal inspired much more powerful emotions than the relocated hall itself. When the first guests entered the renovated Kaisersaal, a subtle sense of disappointment was palpable. Had this room, with its faux pomp and restored façade ornamentation, really been worth so much money and effort? Never mind. It had, in any event, survived both the war and construction.

But back to the Daimler project on the other side of Potsdamer Platz. The opening ceremony took place on 2 October 1998 – on the eve of the anniversary of German reunification. The only noteworthy thing about the lacklustre speech given by Daimler's new CEO Jürgen Schrempp was the fact that he didn't so much as mention his predecessor Edzard Reuter, who had acquired the property before the fall of the Wall. Apparently Schrempp couldn't bring himself to share credit with his predecessor for the success of inaugurating the new city section. And where was the project's prophetic inventor, Edzard Reuter, during this celebration? A Daimler insider told me that Jürgen Schrempp had disinvited Reuter, who had already been asked to join as guest of honour. Deeply hurt, Reuter steered clear of the event.

From the moment Jürgen Schrempp took over as CEO he broke off all contact with his predecessor. The insider told me he thought Schrempp was never able to forgive Reuter for having failed to brief him, before a shareholders' meeting in 1995, about a profit warning that was due to be issued. But the falling-out may also have simply been the result of the cultural distance between the two men. Schrempp, a former car mechanic from Freiburg in Baden-Württemberg, had risen to the head of the group under Reuter's aegis. With his chummy manner he had won even the trust of this rather reserved Berlin intellectual and mayor's son. Reuter then found himself at a loss when Schrempp suddenly wanted nothing more to do with him and asked him not to attend the christening of Reuter's own brainchild. During his years in office, Schrempp made a determined effort to rid himself of the neighbourhood that had been inspired by his predecessor.

In late 2012 I visited Manfred Gentz, whom I had met at the start of the construction works and grown to appreciate, at his office in Haus Huth. (By this point, the prefix 'Wein' had been eliminated from the word 'Haus'.) The immaculately renovated building sits like a museum piece from the *Gründerzeit* – the period of rapid industrial expansion and economic growth in Germany at the end of the 19th century – between Renzo Piano's high-rises with their yellow screen cladding. When I rang the buzzer, a voice answered asking who was there and what I wanted. In the hallway, after passing through an automatic door, I found myself in front of a brand-new elevator. This building, where I had witnessed so much hullabaloo, seemed quiet now, downright forlorn – as did Manfred Gentz, who had directed the giant Potsdamer Platz project. I asked him how it was possible that the Daimler project had been sold just a few years after being completed. He had always considered the sale a mistake, Gentz replied with a barely audible trace of melancholy in his voice. The decision had been related primarily

THE PASSENGER   Peter Schneider

to changes in the capital market. The new evaluation criteria had pushed companies to reduce their required operating capital as much as possible so they could report higher returns; the more capital was tied up, the smaller the returns.

Daimler had invested some two billion Deutschmarks ($1 billion) in the Potsdamer Platz project. Inevitably, there were big write-offs on the investment during the first few years; it was only after ten to fifteen years that the group broke even and began to make a profit. Jürgen Schrempp had never made a secret of his aversion to Berlin and to the Daimler project in the city. Investment bankers kept at him with their philosophy of reducing tied-up capital and convinced him it was essential to get rid of Potsdamer Platz as quickly as possible. But it was only in 2008, when rents and real-estate prices in Berlin were completely depressed, that it was finally sold to a real-estate fund of the Swedish banking group SEB.

Haus Huth, where the Daimler group's Berlin representatives had their own headquarters, had also been sold. Renting the building is probably more expensive than the cost of depreciation would have been if Daimler had held on to it. As Gentz saw me out, he allowed himself a little laugh as he remarked that, after years of creating and supervising the Daimler project at Potsdamer Platz, he was now a guest in his own house.

In the meantime, the Sony Center, which was initially sold to Morgan Stanley, had also changed hands again. In 2010 it was acquired by a Korean pension fund for 573 million euros. No one is talking about a profit. The displaced-at-great-expense Kaisersaal serves as a café, gourmet restaurant and lounge for special events – more than anything, it lives on the fame of how it got to its new location. It sits at the edge of Helmut Jahn's plaza like a befuddled temple. It still seems to be asking itself: How did I end up here; what in the world am I doing here?

I don't consider Potsdamer Platz a masterpiece of modern urban architecture. Too many disparate demands, interests and mentalities acted as midwives to the project. The prescribed pace and the pressure to adhere to standards guaranteeing immediate public success – casino, shopping mall, fountains – produced an aesthetic of the lowest common denominator. In fact, two very distinct sections have emerged on the former wasteland in the middle of Berlin. What these two sections, both established by major corporate groups, have in common is the fact that they have absolutely nothing to do with the old Potsdamer Platz. Not with the Potsdamer Platz of the 1920s, not with the Potsdamer Platz of the post-war years, not with the desert that reigned here during the years of the Wall.

What was it that my city guide Wolf Jobst Siedler had said? 'You'll find you often have to decide what matters more to you: the beauty of a place or its liveliness!' A beauty Potsdamer Platz is not. But it's definitely lively! ✒

Excerpts as adapted from 'Potsdamer Platz' from *Berlin Now: The City After the Wall* by Peter Schneider, translated by Sophie Schlondorff. Translation copyright © 2014 by Sophie Schlondorff. Reprinted by permission of Farrar, Straus and Giroux and Penguin UK.

Der Himmel Unter Berlin

The 1990s saw a generation of young people experiencing Berlin as a wild frontier, one they could explore and make their own. They occupied abandoned buildings, transforming them into clubs of legend, and anything seemed possible. It was in this climate of incurable optimism that the native Berliner and DJ Ellen Allien began to play her part in the development of what was to become the soundtrack of those years: techno.

CHRISTINE KENSCHE
Translated by Stephen Smithson

Left: A portrait of Berlin-based DJ Ellen Allien.
(Photograph by Jordi Perez)

BOOM
BOOM
BOOM

BOOM
BOOM
BOOM

It was one of those nights at the E-Werk, or perhaps it was already daylight, when Ellen Allien first got a sense of her own power. She had just put on a record – massive bassline, stripped-back sound:

Ellen held on to the repetitive rhythm for a few minutes more before letting the hi-hat slam into the hall. Suddenly people began to scream – sound, light, ecstasy. She looked up from her turntables. In that moment she learned how it works, how a crowd is brought to a climax.

BOOM
BOOM
BOOM

BOOM
BOOM
BOOM

A fog of dry ice was billowing white along the factory floor; brightly coloured scarves were hanging down from the ceiling; laser light shot through the high space and bounced off the tiled walls back into the damp air. Flashes lasting fractions of a second lit up sweating bodies moving silently to the hard beats.

That summer of 1995 promised to be hot. Forecasts were for record numbers of sunny days, clear blue skies and scarcely any rain. No need to carry your passport with you on holiday either, since the long-planned Schengen Agreement had finally

CHRISTINE KENSCHE studied history, political science and German studies in Bonn and Rome before working as a journalist reporting from Italy, Israel, Gaza and the West Bank for various German news outlets. She is currently the Middle East correspondent for *Die Welt*.

come into effect that spring. Germany, France, Belgium, the Netherlands and Luxembourg had already dismantled their border controls, and now Spain and Portugal had announced that they, too, would from now on be allowing travellers to pass unhindered. Whereas to the west the horizon seemed to stretch out indefinitely, from the east the next storm was brewing. The parliament in Bonn had just approved an operation by the Bundeswehr in Bosnia, and now Germany would be carrying out its first military operation since the end of the Second World War. But here in Berlin all of that was far, far away. The communist GDR had been shut down, and in its former territory a party was still going on that had started the night the Wall fell. The party had yet to reach its high point, and nobody was ready to go home; the dreariness of the Cold-War era was a long way from having been sweated out of the system.

Ellen Allien could still feel that dreariness clogging her every pore. Unlike many at this long party, she was a real Berliner. She had grown up in a high-rise estate in Tempelhof, south of the airport of that name, which at the time, the 1970s, was under US control. Her mother had raised her and her older sister on her own. Occasionally the girls would stay at their grandma's place in Lichtenrade, right next to the Wall. One night they heard a loud crackling whipping along the street. 'Shooting heard at the Wall again,' they read the next morning on the front page of *Berliner Zeitung* down at the kiosk.

In West Berlin the war had been at its coldest. On the way to her grandma's she would see soldiers patrolling. Now and then a tank would roll past; military hardware would thunder through the estate. A heaviness hung over the city like the smell of the Rekord lignite briquettes that she breathed in when she opened the window of her childhood bedroom. One of her sister's friends installed jukeboxes in bars, and he would bring her the discarded records. When her mother was out of the house, she would place her speakers on the windowsill facing out into the courtyard so that the neighbours could hear their new music. On Fridays her sister would sometimes take her along to a youth club. The doorman would turn a blind eye; he lived in the same block. Inside the club the sounds of the charts would spin around and around – Madonna, Whitney Houston and particularly Michael Jackson. Once, when the DJ played some Kraftwerk, she felt the sound burrowing into her synapses and altering the pulse of her brainwaves. Music was something physical, a channel through which vibrations were produced and feelings intensified. It produced a tingling in the palms of her hands, and it described moods in ways that words never could; it was the measure of the world, and it also made that world more intense. Music expanded the space within her and blasted away all anxiety into a space outside her.

After leaving school she had fled the narrowness of the divided city. She moved to London, found a job as a nanny and enjoyed the limitless freedom of nightlife. In Soho nightclubs she heard acid house for the first time. The slam of the bass drum carried her away like nothing she had ever danced to in West Berlin youth-club discos. As if it were firing the starting shot for a new age in which all previously known rhythms dissolved to flow into a composite sound that were discomfiting while also promising so much. After a year she put her new records in her suitcase and returned home to her boyfriend who, with a few others, had occupied a house in Schöneberg that had been standing empty. He had set up a small studio for himself

'This energy, this optimism – that comes from the fall of the Wall. Suddenly everything was possible, overnight. That's when I created my playground.'

on the first floor in which he produced African bands, and the musicians shared an apartment above. A few weeks later she was lying on the homemade wooden loft bed when her boyfriend called over to her from the kitchen, 'They're saying on the radio that the Wall has been opened.' She yelled back, 'Are you kidding me?'

Gloomy – that was her first impression of the city on the other side of the Wall. She went on bicycle safari: Friedrichshain, Prenzlauer Berg, Mitte – façades perforated by bullet holes, aged streets patched up with tar.

Pale-yellow trams crawled past sooty-brown houses. Trams were not something she had seen in the West – nor was this lack of light. Nowhere was there the blink or flash of advertising, and even the street lights cast more shadow than light on the broad pavements, their cones glimmering faintly orange against the dusk. This eastern Berlin was a different planet.

At night she would stand behind the counter in the Fischlabor and sell bottled Space Beer with labels that glowed in the dark. This Schöneberg bar was one of the first places in Berlin to play techno – acid house from the UK, deep house from Chicago and, above all, the hard techno sound from Detroit. Sometimes Ellen would play a tape she'd mixed herself. She would experiment, intercut passages and sample without having much idea of the technology. Ecki the bartender called her 'my Ellien' because he thought her music sounded like the first *Alien* film – mystical somehow, from another universe. One evening, before any guests had turned up,

she was sitting at the bar with Ecki when an organiser came in from E-Werk, one of the city's biggest new techno clubs. 'I want you to DJ at my place,' he said to her. 'I can't DJ at your club. I've never played in front of people. I can't.' 'You can. What's your DJ name? I'll just put you on the flyer.' 'No, really, I can't ...' 'Allien,' Ecki butted in. 'Ellen Allien! But "Allien" with a double L!'

She still uses the name to this day, although she's now come to think it sounds a little silly. It appears in bold letters on the line-ups of summer festivals in Ibiza, Morocco and Brazil. It stands for the Berlin feel – wild and free. This Berlin is already a thing of the past. Sometimes she will mix sections from earlier pieces into her sets, reminders of the pioneering days of techno – but no sense of recognition flickers on the faces of her fans; they did not live through this period. The crowd in front of the mixing desk is always the same age; only Ellen gets older. But when she plays she looks young. She jumps back and forth behind the turntables, spreads her arms as though she were flying. Her blonde hair bounces in time to the music; she wears it girlishly in a plait. Over the inside of her left forearm an Alien tattoo stretches, her trademark.

The alarm clock usually rings in the middle of the night. She has become used to sleeping in bursts, nodding off in the airport, taking a shower in the lounge. But no matter how tired she is, the stylus only has to hit the record and she's spinning into life again. Rest breaks don't feature in her life; she has to keep moving – like a marathon runner, as she says of herself. Perhaps

ELLEN ALLIEN

To this day Ellen Allien (above, in a photograph taken in the early 1990s) is at the forefront of the development of electronic music in her native city and across the world. Over the years her label BPitch Control has continued to influence the underground electronica scene and remains one of the genre's most important international platforms. Drawing on a mix of music and street culture, the globetrotting Berlin DJ has also launched her own fashion collection and experimented in different media, including visual art. In 2018, inspired by her creative drive and constant search for new sources of inspiration, Ellen Allien came up with a new record label by the name of UFO Inc. The label serves as an incubator for raw techno, encapsulating the holistic, intuitive approach of a musician constantly looking to the future.

this is because everything was once so static, the road blocked every which way you tried to move. 'This energy,' she says, 'this optimism – that comes from the fall of the Wall. Suddenly,' she snaps her fingers, 'everything was possible, overnight. That's when I created my playground.'

The old order no longer existed, but there was no sign of a new one. Looking for places to have a little fun, young people with torches and crowbars wandered across the former death strip and found sites for clubs they opened with names like Bunker, E-Werk and Tresor – each telling of its recent past. The armoured vaults of what was then the Wertheim department store on Leipziger Platz, for example, had been used by the Globus travel bank as a safe deposit. Between the iron bars and the rusty safe-deposit boxes was now a dance floor. The mixing desk was on an old brewery table; cigarette smoke would grow dense under the low ceiling; sweat would drip down; glasses of lukewarm beer would be passed through the grille. Sometimes the cigarette lighters would cease to work because the oxygen had all been used up. The need for ventilation had not occurred to anybody.

When the police came, which seldom happened, somebody would show a paper with several official-looking stamps on it – this was falsified, but in a place where nobody could say what belonged to whom and whose rules were in force this did not matter. The imploded GDR had been turned into a Temporary Autonomous Zone, the title of a book current on the scene by American philosopher Hakim Bey setting out the notion of a short-lifespan zone in which social rules and power relations are suspended – a space of possibility that remains open for just as long as it takes before property relations become clarified and investors wake up. In Berlin the utopia

Above: Floating bars on the Flutgraben
with the legendary Club der Visionäre easily
recognisable.
Below: Concert posters in Alexanderplatz.
Below right: The entrance to Klunkerkranich,
the bar on the roof of the Neukölln Arcaden
shopping centre.

Above: Live music during the Sunday flea market at the Mauerpark.
Below: 'Abandon hope all ye who enter here' – queuing to get into Berghain.

was becoming reality. It was the hour of the anarchists, who took over this fallow period and, to celebrate the freedom won so unexpectedly, held a festival at which nothing would count except the here and now – a peaceful revolution made by ravers. Techno was the soundtrack of this extraordinary time.

Ellen heard about her city's new coordinates while she was in Fischlabor. There she met people who showed her the way to a wartime bunker, the ruins of a department store and a substation at the former Reich Aviation Ministry. Her heart was in her mouth as she walked down a flight of stairs, going further below ground, into the dark, towards a dull thudding that slowly grew louder until a door opened and strobe flashes flickered in her face while strawberry-scented fog filled her lungs and the beat thrummed in her ears. The music was metallic, raw and dirty – just like the club, which took it to another dimension. Time and space dissolved; your mind drifted away, handing control to your body, which danced and danced until euphoria flooded all its cells.

In hip-hop clubs you'd get the odd hand on your backside and the occasional voice talking dirty in your ear. The songs were about hard men and easy women; the atmosphere was sultry and sexist. But here she could move freely, and it felt safe to let her body go into a trance. And moving, not pulling, was what it was about. At the techno parties you didn't get anyone standing on the periphery trying to look as cool as possible; people came for the ecstasy. At 120 beats per minute it's impossible to dance correctly, so it's also impossible to dance incorrectly. Dress codes didn't exist; because everyone was sweating, the clothes were functional. The music had no words, no message; everyone could rediscover themselves in it. She had

shaved her hair short and dyed it peroxide blonde, wore jeans and baggy T-shirts. Every weekend she got to know new people – kids from the East who had been turned away from the chic clubs in the West, gays who smooched on the dance floor, hooligans, squatters, ex-punks, soldiers on leave. All the people who no longer wanted anything to do with the German depression. Everyone was equal, free and united in the feeling of being part of an unrepeatable moment.

Many of her new friends came from eastern Berlin. In the clubs they could shake off the musty odour of standardised, Party-approved youth culture. No more 'record entertainers' forcing politically conformist hits on them; now everyone was allowed to play whatever they wanted. Down here in the basement the politics of the world above had no part to play, and there was no talk of *Wessi* superiority or *Ossi* moaning. The organisers were *Ossis*, the DJs *Wessis* or vice versa. Flyers promised an 'exit from reality', and new drugs helped facilitate that journey. Ecstasy, colourful pills, supplied the energy needed for dancing all the way. At Sunday lunchtime, having emerged from one of these basements, a roaring in her ears and the blinding daylight in her eyes, she would sometimes drive off with her new friends back to an apartment belonging to one or other of them; here amid furnishings that were always the same, no matter which apartment it was, they would hang out. None of them ever had any money; everything was bartered. The GDR had provided them with steady jobs as locksmiths, clerical workers, bookbinders. What would become of them?

Ellen tried to keep her head above water by sticking to music and everything connected to it in any way. Four days a week she worked at Delirium, a record store in Wilmersdorf where those in the

'People came for the ecstasy. At 120 beats per minute it's impossible to dance correctly, so it's also impossible to dance incorrectly. Dress codes didn't exist; because everyone was sweating, the clothes were functional. The music had no words, no message.'

techno vanguard would gather to check out the latest trends. On Thursday evenings she had her own radio show on Kiss FM. At weekends she would DJ at the Fischlabor, at E-Werk and at Tacheles. To this list was soon added Tresor, where she would DJ every Sunday and would sometimes also put in time on the door or on the cash desk. While clearing up afterwards here she got to see the brutal side of nightlife. From the darker corners of eastern Europe a mafia emerged, demanding protection money from the clubs. One evening she overheard a couple of Russians using threats to get the organiser to hand over the door money. When he refused they beat him to the ground. He got up again, wanting to show his strength; they knocked him down again. Friends grabbed Ellen by the arm saying, 'You can't do anything now.' She held her breath, hoping he would just lie there, but he pulled himself up again, blood oozing from his cheeks, only for them to hit him in the face again.

Such scenes toughened a person up. Slight though she was, and rather shy, she quickly came to realise that modesty would not get her very far. Because only a few women in the industry made their own music, she always enjoyed a lot of attention at the DJ booth, although 'enjoyed' is the wrong word here. She was so nervous during her early appearances that her shaky hand caused the needle to jump on the vinyl. She wondered what the others thought of her, the older DJs who treated her like their little sister, quietly smiling

as they watched her DJ and sharing some of their tricks with her. Her sets weren't as hard as the men's, with less reliance on steady beats. She liked stylistic juxtapositions and wild mixes, the main consideration being that it should all hang loose and that the rhythm should have balls. She danced along while she twisted the knobs in the miniature cosmos she had created out of sound. Sometimes she would look at people, and she liked it when they closed their eyes; it made her feel as though they were all floating together. In time she came to recognise the faces at the front. She had built up a fan club whose members followed her from gig to gig.

During one Love Parade (see the sidebar on page 41) she broadcast her radio programme live from Tresor for sixty hours. Increasingly people would come up to the desk to ask for recordings, as though they were reaching to hold on to the moment and postpone the here and now a little longer. Did they feel that the window of the Temporary Autonomous Zone was gradually closing? The police were now carrying out regular raids, and they wanted to see proper permits. As investors competed desperately for building space in the new centre of Berlin, clubs were forced to shut down or move, their place taken by office complexes that shot up into the sky. The few hundred who danced behind the Love Parade cars at the start had grown into hundreds of thousands. Camel and Puma were now sponsors. Marusha's 'Somewhere Over the Rainbow'

'More and more tourists came wanting to visit the techno capital and see what remained of the playground of post-communist anarchy.'

was their anthem, and, with this track, techno stormed the charts. The sell-out of the underground had begun, and new professions had now grown up out of the scene: the hobbyists were now operating as producers, the people who had always put together the flyers for parties became designers and the lad who had helped get the gig ready was now a booker.

If you wanted to continue playing you had to aim for the next level. In 1995 Ellen founded her own label, Braincandy. She bought a fax machine and wrote sales orders on the floor. After two years she was bankrupt. She had produced too much and sold too little. GEMA, the German government's agency for collecting music rights, wanted to see money; her radio show was dropped. She had been floating in a bubble, but now it had burst and reality was streaming in. How was she to pay the outstanding bills? She felt her family's scepticism – DJ? What kind of job was that? Friends visited the clubs less and less often; they had children or got qualifications; all suddenly had demanding jobs. The party was over, and the day – this everyday life – was so sober, so full of rules and fixed processes. Seen in the cold light of day she *was* an alien. She saw the others marching along, and although she couldn't bring herself to get in line with them and didn't want to, she did find herself wondering how things were supposed to go from here. She thought about embarking on a degree, but what she was really good at was partying, making people dance. She had to keep moving somehow. She organised a series of events, to which she invited DJs

who had become friends, while colleagues from abroad also came by. Often they would be headed off at the mixing desk by young people. 'Just give this a listen,' they would say, passing mixtapes to her. 'It must be possible to make something out of all this,' friends urged. 'You have so many contacts.' And so she tried again. In 1999 everything would get better.

In the Bundestag they were just packing the last of the boxes labelled simply 'Bonn–Berlin'. Under the July moon, trains rolled between the old and new capitals every night, forty containers per delivery. They were reloaded at Lehrter station: 120,000 pieces of furniture, thirty-eight kilometres of files, 46,000 boxes of books and the inventory of several in-house printing presses made their way from there to the government district nearby. The MPs set up their offices, while a long queue formed in front of the freshly cleaned sandstone façade of the Reichstag. Express lifts carried people in groups to the domed glass roof; the visitor service recorded almost sixty thousand people in the first few days after the opening. Until late into the night they queued to go up, when the skyline was studded with lights from the construction sites showing the extent of that week's activity. While the grand politics was moving back in, German soldiers were moving out again; in Kosovo they were now firing at Serbian armed forces' radar positions. Joschka Fischer defended the deployment and spoke of another Auschwitz; then the 'warmonger' of the left was hit on his right ear by a bag of red paint.

THE PASSENGER   Christine Kensche

LOVE PARADE

In 1989 the DJ Dr. Motte had the brilliant idea of organising an electronic-music parade along West Berlin's iconic shopping street, the Ku'damm, registering it as a peace protest or, more accurately, a protest for *Friede, Freude, Eierkuchen* ('peace, joy and pancakes', a German saying). Thanks to its status as a political demonstration, the 150 participants in the first ground-breaking Love Parade on 1 July 1989 were able to dance with a police escort rather than being forcibly removed, as could be the case with illegal parties. The sound systems on the floats were synchronised, playing the same three ninety-minute cassettes. By the second parade the crowd had already swelled to two thousand, growing to as many as five thousand in 1991, by which time the Love Parade was no longer just a Berlin event, as young people began to arrive from all over Germany. In 1999 (the year that *The Passenger* editor Marco Agosta took the photographs above), the event attracted a record-breaking 1.5 million people. Not since the days of Hitler had such vast crowds marched through Berlin. The parade helped both to popularise electronic music and to launch the image of Berlin as the movement's global capital, inspiring many other similar events. As the years went by divisions grew among the original core group of organisers over the commercialisation of the Berlin party, and a counter-parade was established, known as the Fuckparade. After the peak in 1999 interest in the Love Parade waned year on year, until the decisive split came in 2003, when the figurehead Dr. Motte also abandoned ship. Two years later new organisers took over and moved the parade to the Ruhr, the scene of the 2010 tragedy that signalled the end, when twenty-one people were crushed to death in the crowd in Duisburg.

Ellen took in the events of that summer out of the corner of her eye, with BPitch Control, her new label, requiring all her attention. This time she made use of her network, producing the first records by Sascha Funke and Paul Kalkbrenner, two eastern German DJs who soon became known worldwide. Electro 'Made in Berlin' was the new stamp of quality, a German export with a wider reach than surface-to-air missiles. The noise from the impact started as a swelling buzz. At some point Ellen was sitting on the tram when the voices around her crept into her consciousness: Swabian, Italian, Spanish, French, English – a babel-like confusion.

More and more tourists came wanting to visit the techno capital and see what remained of the playground of post-communist anarchy. International magazines raved about Berlin's nightlife, which still had no curfew. Berlin was poor but sexy, announced Klaus Wowereit, then Berlin's mayor. Word of the Berlin panacea made its way around: 'Here you can be free – free and wild.' The low rents attracted artists, people who wanted to do something in music or the media, young gays breaking out of their Catholic villages in southern Europe ...

They changed the face of the city. The sooty brown of the old façades disappeared under paint rollers; coal stoves were discarded; pubs and small shops were transformed into bars and studios. There were complaints about rising rents and the hordes of tourists; these came mostly from people who had moved there themselves years ago. Ellen did not lend her voice to this chorus. She recalled only too well how dreary West Berlin had been when it was like a provincial town that hardly anyone wanted – or was even allowed – to visit. Her home was now a desirable destination, a world city like New York or Paris. Just cooler. The dance floors in the clubs were filling up again, and suddenly she started to find enquiries from Tokyo, Barcelona and London in her mailbox. She was able to buy an apartment and take on staff. She took drugs only on rare occasions; she needed a clear head to face the new challenges and keep track of business.

One Monday morning as she headed home, her record case under her arm, and watched the people carrying briefcases to work she felt the energy again, that optimism. She wasn't an alien any longer. She belonged to Berlin, like night to day. The first track she put out on her new label was called 'Stadtkind' ('Child of the City'). It has a fast beat and lyrics:

The night
is over;
a new day
begins;
everything
flows.
Berlin,
you give me
the power;
I am part
of you. ⬎

Ellen Allien in front of the dilapidated Haus der Statistik, the former headquarters of the GDR's statistics agency, built in 1970 and empty since 2008. (Photograph by Marie Staggat)

Ufo

This was the first club in Berlin to play acid house at the end of the 1980s and to open its doors to techno. It was the favourite meeting place for the scene's core of dedicated pioneers, who experimented with a new way of dancing, interacting and being together, trying to distance themselves from the norms of traditional discos. There was no selection at the door and no stars were invited. Inside, there was no stage, and the DJ played in the middle of the crowd. An underground venue in all senses of the word, it was in a cellar with a ceiling only 1.9 metres high and accessed only through a small window on 6 Köpenicker Strasse in Kreuzberg. After the police discovered it, Ufo moved to Schöneberg, where it remained until its final party, held on New Year's Eve 1991.

Tekknozid

In East Berlin, too, there were people interested in the new electronic music who liked breakdancing and listened in secret to Monika Dietl's cult West Berlin radio programmes. Alongside DJ Marusha, Dietl is seen as the first to have spread the techno gospel on the radio and give listeners coded messages about parties going on in the city, most of which were illegal. A few weeks after the fall of the Wall, DJ Wolle XDP organised the first ever house night in East Berlin and then promoted a series of parties called Tekknozid, a meeting of techno and acid house. These were seminal events

inspired by British raves, held in one big room lit only by strobe lights, with no stage or bar. One of the regulars was Tanith, considered to be the hardest of the early techno DJs, who began the rave fashion for camouflage clothing.

Tacheles

This cultural centre, a symbol of 1990s Berlin, saved the building in which it is housed from being demolished in an almost miraculous way. It was built in 1909 as a department store on Friedrichstrasse. By the time of the Cold War, the former Jewish quarter of Scheunenviertel where the building is located (very close to the Oranienburger Strasse synagogue), was a dilapidated zone of East Berlin. Having survived the war the building was partly demolished in 1980, and the East Berlin authorities had fixed a date for completing the demolition in April 1990. But a group of artists and activists took advantage of the anarchic climate that followed the fall of the Wall to occupy the building and set up home there, opening studios, a cinema and a venue on the ground floor where some of East Berlin's first techno nights were held. Despite the fact that Tacheles had single-handedly revived this depressed zone, leading to the transformation of Oranienburger Strasse into an area of bars and restaurants heaving with tourists, it was evacuated in 2012 and sold to an American company that remodelled the whole area and promised that part of the building would be used for cultural purposes.

Tresor

This temple of techno was founded in
1991 by the former managers of Ufo.
Looking for a new location in former
East Berlin, Achim Kohlberger and
Johnnie Stieler discovered a building
on Leipziger Strasse, now home to the
biggest shopping centre in Germany
but at that time almost empty. The
biggest surprise was a ladder leading
down to an underground room unused
for forty years, which had served as
the vault for the Wertheim department
store. This dark, claustrophobic
space was perfectly suited to techno's
military aspect. The walls were two
metres thick and two metres high – or
rather two metres low. In 1991 Dimitri
Hegemann, who still runs the club today
from its new premises on Köpernicker
Strasse, founded the Tresor music
label, an important element in the
success of this electronica institution.

Planet

In the early 1990s Planet provided techno fans with an alternative to Tresor. More cheerful, playful, gay friendly and relaxed, it suited those who didn't like the crude sound and atmosphere of the former vault. Resident DJs included the founder of Love Parade, Dr. Motte, who played marathon sets of up to twelve hours. It lasted from 1991 until 1993 in a former factory on Köpernicker Strasse (and also for a short while on the Alt-Stralau peninsula) that later became the venue for the Kater Holzig club.

Mayday

Mayday was an annual indoor electronica event. The first was in 1991, held in the Halle Weissensee in former East Berlin, and it was a meeting point between the idealists and the gradual commercialisation of the movement. Instead of the endless psychedelic sets that were still common at the time, Mayday was a series of star turns, with lots of DJs playing for an hour each. Guest DJs included Marusha and Westbam, both early arrivals on the scene who subsequently achieved success in the charts.

Walfisch

Considered to be one of Berlin's best after-hours venues, Walfisch was the destination for dedicated partygoers after Planet and Tresor closed at about 7 a.m. But these weren't the only people who made up the club's diverse clientele: as well as ravers, it wasn't unusual to find punks, prostitutes, hooligans and British soldiers stationed in Berlin. Consumption of synthetic drugs became increasingly common at these venues, and East Germans – who didn't even know what drugs were and who, until a year before, hadn't been able to organise a musical event unless it had a political or social purpose and was endorsed by the Politburo – were suddenly flung into this parallel world where there were no rules, curfews or limitations. Located in a room next to the Heinrich Heine Strasse metro station, Walfisch was replaced in 1997 by the Sage and KitKat clubs.

Bunker

Walking along Reinhardtstrasse in Mitte, it's impossible to miss this block of reinforced concrete built in 1942 as an air-raid shelter for Berliners. During the GDR years it was used to store dried exotic fruits imported from Cuba, and by the 1990s it inevitably attracted people from the techno scene, always on the lookout for alternative, evocative locations. Here they found bass reverberation like nowhere else, and the sound was even harder and faster than at Tresor, becoming more like gabber or hardcore. Regulars at the legendary venue included Michael Teufele and

Norbert Thormann, the future founders of Ostgut and Berghain, who organised gay parties there. After four years of illegal parties, in 1996 Bunker was closed down, to the dismay of many, and for years afterwards the Fuckparade (see the sidebar on page 41) terminated right in front of the bunker in protest. Since 2003 the former air-raid shelter has been owned by the entrepreneur and art collector Christian Boros, who has built himself a penthouse there with a rooftop swimming pool. Visitors can now visit the rest of the building by appointment to view his art collection.

E-Werk

After all the claustrophobic cellars and bunkers, E-Werk was the first electronica venue designed on a larger scale for a wider public. It was founded in 1993 by the owners of Planet in an evocative venue – a former electrical substation built in the 1920s – in Mitte, not far from Tresor. Gradually, traditional elements crept back in: a stage, star DJs, a backstage area, a divide between regular punters and other groups. E-Werk confirmed Berlin's association with electronica, hosting the best DJs of the time, and MTV even had a party there. Techno was no longer a secret known only to the few. A new phenomenon typical of the 1990s developed in front of the dilapidated building, something that had already been seen at Walfisch, so-called parking-lot raves at which people danced to music pumping out of their car stereos.

We Were Like Brothers

In former East Germany, in the years following reunification, you could find yourself fleeing from neo-Nazi violence but still have friends on the extreme right: one did not preclude the other. Is that still the case today?

DANIEL SCHULZ
Translated by Eric Rosencrantz

Left: The flags of Germany and the Oberhavel district of Brandenburg fly at a farm in Velten, north-west of Berlin.

You can get a kick out of your own ugliness. Embrace it. See the horror on the faces of those watching and despising you but afraid to confront you, and feel the power flowing through your veins like an electric current.

Zipping down the motorway at over a hundred kilometres an hour and pissing on the bonnet of a BMW behind us, I feel the power. Standing there in the open sunroof with my trousers dangling around my thighs and my dick in my hand, I see the driver's eyes widen with horror and outrage. His big pale face blows up like a balloon. I'd like to stick a needle in it.

I'm nineteen years old, ten metres tall and eight metres wide: invincible.

On 27 August 2018, when men of my generation – around forty years old – held a 'funeral march' in Chemnitz and some of them stuck their naked backsides out for the cameras, as you can see on YouTube, I thought about that ride down the *Autobahn*. Watching as big burly guys give Nazi salutes and attack people whose skin colour rubs them up the wrong way, while the cops don't do a thing about it, I'm paralysed, as though something dark were welling back up inside me, something I thought I'd left behind. But I remember that power

trip, too, the thrill of making it plain to someone: 'Rules? What if I don't give a shit about your rules, my friend? What then?'

I see Chemnitz and wonder, 'What have you got to do with me? What have I to do with you?' (For more on this see the sidebar on page 57.)

WINNERS OF THE 1990S

On German Unification Day some will tell you why reunification has been such a success. The very word 'reunification' is a lie, others will counter, pointing out what was lost: companies, self-respect, whole lives. But the yea-sayers come through particularly loud and clear. 'Come on, acknowledge what we've achieved; we had to build a whole new world for ourselves. Give your tales of woe and victimhood a rest.' They'll often add, 'We're proud of what we've accomplished, even if we've failed.'

My parents' and grandparents' generations are telling their stories these days, three decades after the fall of the Wall. It may not be the first time, but it does seem the right time. The Saxon state minister for integration, Petra Köpping, has worked some of these stories into her book *Integriert doch erst mal uns!* ('Integrate Us First!'), and the house is packed at every reading she gives in eastern Germany these days.

DANIEL SCHULZ is a journalist at the *taz* newspaper, for which he has covered right-wing extremism, terrorism and data protection. From 2010 to 2014 he ran the lifestyle pages of *taz2/ medien,* and today he co-manages the reportage section. 'We Were Like Brothers' was judged essay of the year 2018 by the journalists' association Reporter-Forum e.V. and won the Theodor Wolff Prize for journalism in 2019.

A lot of it is about lost jobs and, yes, this sounds nice and technical, like an easy problem to solve. But in this Prussian nation of full employment called the German Democratic Republic, where work was the meaning of life and the jobless few were called *Assis* ('antisocial elements'), it could also mean: co-workers, brothers, husbands who hanged themselves, siblings and cousins who slowly drank themselves to death, families that now suddenly seethed because some now had more than others. And then everything froze into a dead landscape of cold slag. Women who slaved away to keep their husbands, their children and themselves afloat until there was nothing left of them but the will to 'make it'.

Does anyone still want to hear about the 1990s from the perspective of those who were too old when the Wall came down not to remember the past but too young to have a say in their future? About the decade in which the angry mob now bellowing and giving Nazi salutes grew up?

'I associate the 1990s with personal experiences that are coming back to me lately,' says Manja Präkels. 'And when I travel around Germany I often see the same AfD [Alternative für Deutschland, Alternative for Germany] people who consider themselves the winners of the battles of the 1990s.'

Manja Präkels has written a book called *Als ich mit Hitler Schnapskirschen aß* ('When I Ate Brandied Cherries with Hitler'; Verbrecher, 2017) about the final days of the GDR and the decade of barbarity that eastern Germany experienced afterwards. The author was born in 1974 and grew up in Zehdenick, a town north of Berlin. After Christian Bangel's *Oder Florida* (Piper, 2017) Präkels' was the second autobiographical novel to come out in that year about eastern Germany in the 1990s. I called her

to ask if the images from Chemnitz and Köthen remind her of the old days, too. She said that when she's on a book-signing tour or at conferences, she comes across right-wing extremists who are driven by what they accomplished back then in Rostock-Lichtenhagen and by the many smaller – and mostly unnoticed – fires they managed to start. 'They see themselves as the victors of those battles,' she says, 'because people of colour were evacuated from eastern Germany at the time. In their eyes that legitimised the violence of those years after the fact.'

So where do I begin my story about those dark days? For me it didn't start in 1989; for me it started in East Germany.

A SWASTIKA ON THE SCHOOL DESK

In second grade, Ricardo drew a swastika on his desk with his pencil. That was nothing unusual in and of itself. I'd done that, too, one day in June 1987, while scrawling in my copybook: 'Our mother is coming home late today. We want to help.' Drawing swastikas was the most forbidden thing I could imagine. Every time I did it a little beast inside me roared with joy at not having been caught. The trick is to turn the swastika into a little window before anyone sees it.

But Ricardo was not quick enough that day, or maybe he'd just forgotten to connect up the lines. I saw it, two friends of ours saw it, so we had a word with him while the teacher was out of the classroom. We couldn't tell her; snitching on someone was the worst thing you could do. We had to settle the matter between ourselves.

'You know that was wrong?' I said. He was snivelling. He was heavier and taller than me, but he didn't try anything with two other classmates standing right beside him. 'Take off your glasses,' I said. Ricardo snivelled some more, pleading with his wide eyes. Yeah, sure, we lived in the same housing block, and yeah, we were going to meet up at the sandbox in front of the building that afternoon as usual, but first we had to settle the matter at hand.

Tijan Sila, a writer born in socialist Yugoslavia, describes this boyhood behaviour in *Tierchen Unlimited* ('Little Beasts, Unlimited'; Kiepenheuer & Witsch, 2017) as follows:

> The development of elementary school children was supposed to mirror the ethos of the party, which to me at the time meant only contradictions: above, a cold, lurking Apollonian face that demanded virtue, sobriety, forbearance, and below, a libidinous, demonic torso that favoured cruelty, battle, rivalry and sacrifice. Perhaps this torso was left when the head passed away with East Germany.

NEO-NAZI VIOLENCE PLAYED DOWN AS APOLITICAL HOOLIGANISM

Fighting was writ large in the German Democratic Republic. The greatest fighters were the ones who were no longer around: communist anti-fascists who'd died in the camps so we'd be better off. Brawny white men gazed back at us from school murals and from our illustrated textbooks. All our teachers told us about the Jews was that the National Socialists had killed them off. At any rate, they hadn't put up a fight.

On the way home from school we'd tell jokes about Jews. Four or five of us would walk home together over cobblestones and black sand, past the cemetery and the bar, to the four blocks of new buildings on the outskirts of the village.

One guy says, 'What's the jackpot in the concentration camp lottery?'

I say, 'I've heard that one before: free tickets to the gas chamber.'

THE KEBAB MURDERS

On 4 November 2011 Beate Zschäpe handed herself in to the police after an attempted robbery of the Sparkasse bank in Eisenach, Thuringia. Her accomplices, Uwe Mundlos and Uwe Böhnhardt, had been found dead in a burning camper van. Other discoveries in the vehicle included a service weapon issued to the policewoman Michèle Kiesewetter, who had been killed in 2007. Zschäpe had also set fire to the house where the three lived, in which weapons and evidence were found that enabled the authorities to solve a number of cases dating from between 2000 and 2007. It emerged that they were key members of the neo-Nazi terrorist group the Nationalsozialistischer Untergrund (NSU), which was supported by 100–150 people who supplied them with weapons, money and forged documents. The NSU had not claimed responsibility for its crimes, including two bombings and at least fifteen robberies. The controversies that followed the discovery centred mostly on the fact that the police had attributed the crimes to a settling of scores among immigrants without considering political or racist motives: the victims of the murders had been nine businessmen of foreign origin, eight Turkish and one Greek. Alongside the trial that ended in 2018 with a life sentence for Beate Zschäpe, the German secret services also found themselves in the dock, accused of inefficiency and unreliability as well as collusion. Since reunification there have been 109 murders linked to extreme-right-wing politics, although some believe the true figure could be much higher.

Later on I found our jokes again in *Das hat's bei uns nicht gegeben!* ('That Didn't Happen Here!'), a book published a few years ago by the Amadeu Antonio Foundation, which was named after an Angolan contract labourer who in 1990 got beaten up so badly and for so long by a bunch of youths in Eberswalde that he fell into a coma and eventually died.

Where we got our jokes from I don't recall. There weren't supposed to be any to begin with. The GDR constitution said that fascism had been defeated and, being defeated, it wasn't supposed to exist any more. The State Security Service, it says in the foundation's book as well as in the Stasi's own reports, described swastikas at Jewish cemeteries and neo-Nazi assaults as '*Rowdytum*' ('hooliganism'), as though they had no political dimension. The secret service and police persecuted punks, on the other hand, and anyone who looked different from the socialist establishment's image of the upstanding citizen, as outgrowths of a decadence that could only emanate from the West.

And the AfD are taking up that mindset today. More than any other party, the far-right AfD strives to celebrate and promote an eastern German identity. In election campaigns and speeches, their politicians woo voters by stressing how nice and German things still are in eastern Germany, how little has changed there. And to this day many police officers buy the story about apolitical hooliganism.

AN ALARMING INVESTIGATION IS BURIED

Were things better in West Germany? This is a perennial question that always comes up when writing about East Germany. Well, at least public debate was possible in West Germany. A series like *Holocaust* couldn't be shown on East German TV, people couldn't discuss it, get upset or cry about

it afterwards at home, in a bar, on the bus. And it's understandable that we don't want West Germans interpreting our lives for us any longer, but what is more important: to salvage a whitewashed memory of East Germany or to give some thought to why our own kids are being terrorised by Nazis – or terrorising others themselves?

After neo-Nazis attacked a punk gig at Zionskirche, a church in East Berlin in 1987, the central committee of the SED (Socialist Unity Party) decided to investigate neo-Nazi activities after all. In 1988 investigators counted as many as five hundred offences per month committed by right-wing extremists. The powers that be were so alarmed by the findings that they 'buried' the file. And the leading investigator in the case, a high-ranking police officer, was subsequently kept under Stasi surveillance.

In the fourth grade we read the communist novel *How the Steel Was Tempered* by Nikolai Ostrovsky. It was mandatory reading. With the green schoolbook in front of us on our desks, we took turns reading a few lines aloud in class. A Wehrmacht lieutenant sitting on the outskirts of a Soviet village is watching it burn. He sees a boy playing outside and thinks to himself, 'What's the difference between this child and a German one?' As a sergeant's car comes speeding towards the boy, the Nazi soldier saves him in the nick of time, and they flee together to join the Soviet soldiers. The lieutenant later returns to Germany – now fighting for the Red Army. The Nazi's transformation into a communist takes only five and a half pages, and this abridged version for child readers does a pretty good job of encapsulating East Germany's anti-fascist myth. The state had to punish a few instigators. Then, without lingering on the past, it could enlist the vast majority of the remaining population to build the new state.

Houses in Velten in the state of Brandenburg.

We didn't know much about foreigners. We didn't even know our supposed brothers. 'We show our ties of friendship with the Soviet people,' I wrote on 8 May, VE Day, in my social-studies binder. But we hardly saw any of them, although there were plenty stationed not so very far away. Sometimes a contingent carrying Kalashnikovs on their backs would march past our kindergarten, and we'd press up against the fence to gaze after them. 'Fucking Russians,' said a boy next to me one time. When I asked why, he explained, 'If stupid Hitler hadn't wrecked our army, the Russians wouldn't be here now.' At least that's what his father had told him.

We didn't know who the Jews were. We didn't know who the Russians were either. But we knew who the Nazis were; a Nazi was someone from the West. Capitalism was deemed a preliminary stage of fascism, and there were enough old high-ranking Nazis still holding powerful positions in West Germany to prove the point. When in 1960 the Stasi drew up a list of over fifty sites in the district of Rostock defaced with swastikas, the head of the district administration called them 'provocation from West Germany'. In *Käuzchenkuhle*, one of the most widely read books for youngsters in East Germany, a band of schoolboys solve a case in which a 'stranger', a former SS officer from West Germany, returns to recover Nazi plunder, some looted art he'd buried in a nearby lake. As recently as 2006 the SPD (Social Democrat) interior minister of an eastern German state told me before an interview that the Nazi problem came from the West and, no, this sort of thing didn't happen back in the GDR.

The fall of the Wall broke my heart. I was afraid of the West, of the fascists, afraid that everything I knew might fall apart.

I WANTED WAR

The grown-ups didn't lift a finger. They sat in front of the TV watching the protests. They went on teaching us at school as if everything was perfectly normal. It was clear to me – and to every kid who knew where Matchbox cars came from – that we didn't stand a chance economically. But my father was a lieutenant-colonel in the National People's Army. He once commanded thirty tanks. So where were they now?

I wanted a Chinese solution, I wanted Tiananmen Square in Berlin and Leipzig. When my father, the coward, didn't go out to stop the lunatics out there, I started thinking about how to steal his Makarov army pistol. My plan was to shoot a couple of people in West Berlin and start a war. Because I was sure we'd win that one.

We used our *Begrüssungsgeld* ('welcome money' gifted by the West German government to East German visitors from 1970 to 1989) to drive to Berlin-Spandau. I bought myself a video game at Karstadt, a little blue computer on which to play ice hockey. At each new level the puck got faster and harder to catch. It started with 'beep … beep … beep' then sped up to 'beep-beep … beep-beep … beep-beep' and finally to 'beep-beep-beep-beep-beep-beep'. Mesmerised, I'd stare at the little flashing disc until the world around me only came through in muffled sounds as if through cotton wool. The grown-ups had sold out on me, and I'd sold myself out for a computer game. I was furious, but I had no idea at whom.

'You were in Hitler Youth mode,' a friend of mine recounted two decades later, 'like the boys in the *Volkssturm*' (a national militia raised by the Nazis in the last months of the Second World War). He'd seen enough boys in the Yugoslav wars who'd died through anger, fear and helplessness similar to mine.

A FRIEND–FOE GUIDED MISSILE

In second grade we used to sing:

> *Soldaten sind vorbeimarschiert, die*
> *ganze Kompanie.*
> *Und wenn wir gross sind, wollen wir*
> *Soldat sein so wie sie.*

('Soldiers marched by, the whole
company.
And when we grow up, we want to be
soldiers like them.')

Although there were songs in our
music book about peace in the world and
'*Ein Männlein steht im Walde ganz still und
stumm*' ('A little man stands stock-still and
silent in the forest'). And:

> *Mein Bruder ist Soldat im großen*
> *Panzerwagen,*
> *und stolz darf ich es sagen:*
> *Mein Bruder schützt den Staat.*

('My brother is a soldier in a big
armoured car,
and I can say it with pride:
My brother is protecting the state.')

It was clear who that big brother was
protecting us against: the West. But no one
was protecting me now. I wanted to fight,
but against whom? What is the target of
a missile with a friend-or-foe guidance
system when your own parents have joined
the enemy? Was I the only one who felt this
way? I don't know. I never talked to friends
about it.

The meltdown began on TV. I saw
people crying, stiff, grey, mostly in front
of smokestacks, factory gates, and something was always closing down. Then the
men in the village started falling apart.
On my way home from school I'd see them
sitting by their garages. They used to drive

THE EVENTS IN CHEMNITZ

On 26 August 2018 a fight broke out
during a festival in Chemnitz, in the
state of Saxony, and a man was killed
by two immigrants, one Iraqi and one
Syrian. The reaction from various right-
wing groups was almost immediate,
and a xenophobic demonstration
attracting almost a thousand people
was held in the city, with supporters
including Markus Frohnmaier, a
member of parliament for the far-right
Alternative für Deutschland. The next
day violence flared up again when
another demonstration of six thousand
neo-Nazis, who went on to clash with a
group of a thousand left-wing counter-
protestors, degenerated into a hunt
for foreigners. Firecrackers and other
objects were thrown, while people
gave Nazi salutes – a dozen of them
were subsequently investigated. After
an initial clash, the police intervened
to contain the violence, but even then
around twenty people were injured,
caught between the left-wing and neo-
Nazi demonstrators and the ranks of
the police. Some on the far right are no
longer content simply to demonstrate,
however. On 3 June 2019 Walter
Lübcke, a member of Angela Merkel's
Christian Democratic Party, was
found dead at his home. The 65-year-
old politician had taken a very clear
stance on welcoming migrants and
refugees and had long been the
target of threats. The murder was
committed by right-wing extremist
Stephan Ernst, who admitted that
his act was politically motivated.

cranes, big Russian tractors and combine harvesters. Now they'd joke about their wives, who were trying to keep the families afloat with some cleaning job or other or some job-creation scheme. They'd say, 'The old lady gets on my nerves.' Then they'd drink another schnapps. But often they didn't say a word.

The message we read, saw and heard in the papers and on radio and TV was: East Germans are too dumb to cope with the new world; East Germans are lazy; East Germans are drunk. At first I felt ashamed, then I felt amused watching the shit that was being thrown at us fly. Later I felt proud that 'we' were tougher than the squeamish *Wessis*, who can map their whole life story to causal connections in which there's a good reason for everything and no blind spots. It can be liberating, in a demonic way, to know that only the worst

is expected of you and those around you. But at twelve or thirteen, I didn't see that yet. All I saw was the men in their garages – what the future held in store for me.

THE POLICE BACKED DOWN

My father didn't drink in the garage. He was taken on by the West German Army. In the spring of 1992 they were fired at while inspecting a Soviet base. My father left the army and later sold insurance, like many other men from the police force, the Ministry of State Security and the National People's Army. It was a step down, but it wasn't so hard.

On TV you could see buildings burning that housed Vietnamese contract workers. You could see men throwing flagstones at people. I saw how the police stood there helpless in the face of the angry mob. I saw how they backed down.

'Apparently it is not clear to many in western Germany that there are two generational cohorts in eastern Germany whose collective political experience is based on having overthrown a political system and subsequently forced the new state to back down before their racist will in Hoyerswerda and Rostock.' This is what David Begrich, an expert on right-wing extremism, wrote after the Chemnitz marches in an article widely shared on Facebook. Begrich was there in Rostock-Lichtenhagen; he was one of the people the raucous men were throwing flagstones at.

This new state was receding – in small towns and villages – until the late 1990s. A lot of people my age didn't count on it any more. We all saw the same thing: no police coming to the rescue when thirty skinheads showed up at a youth club and started beating people up, or only two cops would drive up and stay in the car. What were they to do? Get battered themselves? That actually did happen sometimes.

The great power of the *Volkspolizei*, the People's Police, is now broken, and so is that of our teachers. Back in the days of East Germany these authorities could single-handedly derail your whole career – whether or not you got to go to college. Now we laugh in their faces. We laugh till they cry. They're afraid of Germany's new, free youth.

YOU COULD GET KILLED, EASY

Nowadays I often travel to eastern European countries that once used to be socialist, too. When I talk to people my age there about how things fell apart in the 1990s, about the barbarity, the collapse of social constraints – which they often describe in harsher and more hellish terms because it was harsher and more hellish there than in Germany – I find they relate to the police much as I did back then: with a mix of fear and contempt.

The 1990s are over, and the new state has since got its act together. But even now, when, as in Chemnitz, there still aren't enough police on the scene, when officials in Köthen merely record a fanatical right-wing speaker sharing her fantasies of gassing and murdering people instead of immediately intervening in the rally, that sort of thing merely confirms what both the Nazis and their adversaries have discovered: the state does back off.

I learned something else in the years after the Berlin Wall came down, as the list of casualties grew longer and longer: you could get killed, easy. All it takes is a single psycho among a horde of Nazis, one who doesn't like the look of you and just can't help himself, then you're done for. Some guys I knew thought they were safe because they were white. They thought they could hide. But you don't get to decide who's different and who isn't, the Nazis do. Mahmud Azhar and Farid Guendoul were killed, but so were Wolfgang Auch and Horst Hennersdorf.

I was eleven or twelve years old when I first encountered hatred in person. My mother was still working as an agro-chemist, calculating how much fertiliser the yellow crop-duster was to drop on the fields around our village. One day the plane's pilot was sitting in a brown upholstered armchair in our living room, waiting for my mother, and – because I liked him, I thought he was cool, I mean, he was a pilot and all – I asked him what was going to happen with him. He was talking about 'Wall Street Jews' being to blame for all this, he got louder, stirred up, turning beetroot red – first his neck, then his face. I remember it so well because 'Wall Street' didn't mean a thing to me, and, as for Jews, I didn't think there were any left in Germany. The man spewed his rage all over me, but I didn't know its cause or its target.

Velten town centre, near the railway station; the town was famous for manufacturing stoves.

SONS OF THE NAZI CLANS

New rules. I'd have liked to have learned them, had I understood them. Better to take the bus where you might get stuck with a bunch of skinheads? Or better to walk or cycle, in which case you're too slow if they chase you in a car? Others tried to figure out the new world, too. The county town was right wing, the villages left wing, but this neat breakdown immediately crumbled when fifteen, twenty, thirty Nazis showed up to make trouble at a village fair.

A lot of the skinheads were from big families. They grew up with busts of Hitler and imperial war flags in their houses. The sons of the clans whose names were to be feared were four-to-eight years older than me. They patrolled the town in low-slung VW Golfs or on foot. Only they could have possibly understood the code that decided who they went after and who they spared. If they knew you from GDR schooldays, that might be a good thing – or bad if they hadn't liked you even then. When they saw dyed hair or long hair, they saw red. But a long-hair from the 'county town' – which got downgraded to 'small town', by the way, in the mid-1990s – was OK for one night: they'd go after a rival Nazi gang instead because they were from the next village and 'moving in on our turf'.

I only vaguely understood these subtleties in the 1990s. Much of what I've learned is from interviews I conducted for this article. I didn't know any of the important Nazis. I was from the village, far from the centre of power, so I couldn't distinguish between the ones I might have been able to take on without five guys then coming after me and the ones who really would finish me off.

Things just happened to me.

One time I'm on the bus, and three skinheads get on without paying. They're walking past me to the back of the bus. I pretend I'm reading, when suddenly I feel something wet on my face. One of them spat in my face. Before I know it, the shortest of the three presses his thumb into my left cheek and rubs it so hard my teeth hurt. 'You really gotta clean yourself up,' he says in a high-pitched voice. 'Or does Mummy have to run after you all the way to the bus to do it for you?' I probably look like a deer caught in headlights. The three of them almost piss themselves laughing. Shorty's hand reeks of stale tobacco.

Or I'm walking the three kilometres home from school, and a car pulls up next to me with its tyres squealing. I hightail it straight into the field. I can hear them behind me, laughing. I run across soft spring green, heavy clumps of mud sticking to my shoes and falling off. They drive down the road, smoking and watching me run. About a kilometre before the village they step on the gas and disappear.

The boy who used to dis the 'fucking Russians' in the GDR shows me the baseball bat he keeps in his car and where he hides his blank gun under the passenger seat. 'I don't drive anywhere unarmed any more,' he says. 'I'm not an idiot.'

I see the years from 1991 to 1998 as through the frosted glass panel of a train-station toilet. It's hard for me to remember. And it's not just me. 'Sometimes I can't help wondering if I didn't just imagine the whole of the 1990s,' Manja Präkels said to me. 'Even friends who were there couldn't or wouldn't remember.'

I AM PREY

I was short and fat as a kid, but during puberty I shot up. Genetically speaking, I'm a Nazi: nearly 1.9 metres tall, blond, with grey-blue eyes. I lift weights. But I lack the thug gene, the lust for blood. I see that bloodthirsty look in the eyes of the

Nazi-clan sons and their henchmen, and I know I am prey. So I try to disappear, I wear grey, I'm a little grey mouse. God, if only I were shorter.

Hadn't I just been reading about Ernst Thälmann and his comrades – how they died fighting fascism? I didn't want to die, I just wanted to be left alone. I was ashamed of myself. We were all ashamed. 'The 1990s are a big taboo in eastern Germany,' says Manja Präkels. 'That period is weighed down with shame.' We each had our reasons. One guy got fired, never found a job again. Another guy stood behind a curtain secretly rejoicing at the sight of the refugee hostel burning down. And as for me, I was simply a coward.

Otherwise I'd have turned out differently. There were some upstanding anti-fascists, the punks: I knew about them but never saw them in the street. Some women I went to school with and later interviewed for this article told me they weren't afraid. One of them said skinheads from her village usually tried to impress her, adding that she's not sure Nazis were really the worst thugs. It wasn't and still isn't easy to distinguish between those, on the one hand, who wanted to bash some heads in and looked to *Mein Kampf* for justification and those, on the other, who bashed heads in because they found it politically imperative. Violence was normal, so the Nazis were right at home in this normality, like fish in the sea.

I didn't tell my parents anything. That would be snitching. Boys used to work things out between themselves, and I figured we should do that now, too. Besides, nothing happened to me. No teeth knocked out, both eyes still in their sockets. I wasn't dead either. Others told their fathers and mothers. Manja Präkels writes about that in her book – including what many parents answered: just don't provoke them!

WHICH IS THE REAL STORY?

The grown-ups couldn't fathom that the dear little Ricardos, Michaels and Kais from school had morphed into fighting machines. I couldn't have explained it to them either. So they conjured up a parallel world. 'There is no problem of right-wing extremism,' the mayors said when another person got clobbered or killed. I wondered, 'Who's nuts here, them or me?'

'Catastrophe struck the parents, who had to struggle to survive,' said Präkels, 'and they often lost track of their kids in the process.' And a new normality emerged amid constant denials, constant assurances that it's normal for fans to sing the Nazi anthem at youth football matches.

And now? A Saxon minister president who begins by insisting that what happened in Chemnitz wasn't all that bad. An intelligence service chief tells the tabloids that a video of an attack was posted in order to distract from a murder. Which is the real story? Most people believe the chief executive of a German state more than a man of colour telling the story of how he was attacked.

I started secondary school in seventh grade in the autumn of 1991. I rarely hung out with my village friends any longer. I was a cut above them now, at least that's how they saw it or how I thought they saw it. I secluded myself. I'd always liked reading, so I spent even more time reading. Shortly before the Wall came down we moved to another block. I had my own room and didn't have to share a bed with my father and mother any more. That made it easier to hide. When I turned sixteen my parents bought a computer, and I played Ice Hockey Manager on it. These game worlds are untouched by the outside world and controllable. I went out once in a while, resurfacing like a submarine after a long voyage. For years the news at the surface was always the same: either there was trouble or someone told you about trouble.

'He forced his girlfriend to walk the streets and then strangled her with a wire.'

'The other day they nearly wasted a guy by the Havel River.'

'They walked into the youth club with an axe. The girl behind the door got it bad straight off. Only two cops showed up again.'

MY NEW FRIENDS WERE SKINS

I didn't have many friends. I was an idiot from a village. Sure, my mother bought me a pair of Levi's after I'd kept begging her, but on my fat backside the jeans looked like someone had tried to knead my behind into two skinny sausages. I had to wear them all the same. That was an expensive pair of trousers. They laughed at me on the school bus. I was often by myself, which made me a target, so I went out even less.

After three years in secondary school I made other friends.

One of them was a short, skinny fellow who smiled a lot and drove me home when it got late. He said, 'My father was already a rightist. That got him into trouble with the fucking communists.'

Another guy in our clique scowled a lot, but he'd give you a tickle all over when you'd had a rotten day at school. He was for the (neo-Nazi) NPD party and had contacts to a fascist clan in a bigger village nearby.

Plus, there was a copper's son, who was always loud, always messing around, shared generously with everyone and couldn't stand the sight of 'wogs'.

And one guy who was always quite calm, although his mother was always at him, going on about how he mustn't drop off in his schoolwork, mustn't fail, mustn't go under in this new world. At home he listened to CDs by bands like Zyklon-B and Zillertaler Türkenjäger (literally,

'Tyrolean Turk-hunters'). He had the word 'Euthanasie' emblazoned in black letters on the rear window of his car: the band were actually called Oithanasie, but he found it a funny play on words to write the name that way.

We cruised across the country in convoy. To the next McDonald's on the motorway or all the way to the Baltic Sea, Czech Republic, Denmark. The bigger our convoy, the wider our map got.

Two cars are good, four cars are better. Our swarm scared people off. I discovered how cool it can be to scare others shitless instead of being scared shitless yourself. So I pissed on a *Wessi* car behind us.

BÖHSE ONKELZ SOUNDTRACK

Right wing and left wing are a matter of clothes, hairstyle and 'inner attitude', as we used to call it. Hard-core Nazi fashion seeped into secondary school, where many donned green bomber jackets with orange lining. I had long hair and had 'nothing against foreigners'; I thought chasing and roughing them up was fucked up. I'd say that out loud sometimes, and then we'd have a row. I had to run away from Nazis. So, I was a leftie.

We weren't very high up on the food chain of youth gangs. When the musclemen emerged from the gym, those tattooed hulks with martial arts or jail time under their belts, and none of the other guys had any connection to someone who knew someone, then we'd keep a low profile or make ourselves scarce.

But, of course, there was still trouble. One time we wanted to go to a lake on Father's Day. Two of the boys were hell bent on cycling there. 'That's a stupid fucking idea,' we said. 'You'll never make it by yourselves.' But they went through with it. We picked them up later, bleeding by the roadside, and laughed at them.

Böhse Onkelz provided the soundtrack for that period. I hated the band. Their songs about guys killed in action reminded me of the men boozing in their garages. But the lyrics of one Onkelz song sticks in my head to this day: 'We were more than friends / We were like brothers / We sang the same songs / For many years'. It's called 'Nur die Besten sterben jung' ('Only the Best Die Young'), and I liked it, maybe because I missed the communist Young Pioneers, the days we preferred picking up litter and discarded bottles to making each other's lives hell, and because I thought to myself, 'Yes, you really might get killed.'

MY MADE-UP TURKISH FRIEND
I still didn't feel safe. One evening I happened to drive to the car park at the Netto supermarket where we always met up. Only a few of us were there, and we were sitting ducks for a bigger bunch of bruisers from a neighbouring village. One of us took quite a beating. He drove home on his moped all the same, but his head was so swollen from the kicks and blows that he couldn't get his helmet off. He ended up in intensive care.

Some memories stick like splinters and still hurt years later. The Turkish friend I made up was one such. The last time we got together we went to Hungary. We chilled by Lake Balaton and played football. We flung open the doors to our toilets and took pictures of each other crapping. We shaved each other's chest hair. And then we're sitting in a café, I'm reading the paper, I might have read something about an attack, I can't remember. A friend says something about 'bloody wogs', that they had it coming, and I immediately go ballistic, shouting that I have a Turkish friend and he's in hospital in Berlin 'because of people like you'. It was a brief outburst, just a few seconds, and I immediately felt terrible.

Because I lied, I didn't have any Turkish friends, not even friends with Turkish names. Where would I find them anyway? There was only one boy at our school who wasn't white, and his father was an engineer from Angola or Mozambique. Even the ladies I knew from the kebab joint were born in town or in one of our villages. I was also ashamed because I knew there were people who really did get burned or kicked to death. And there I was making one up. And yet at the same time I was afraid our friendship was over.

'Oh shit, is he badly hurt?' my friend asks. I murmur something like 'Not too bad'. I keep lying; once you start you can't just stop. 'I'm sorry,' he says, 'I didn't mean it that way.'

That was another truth about those years: many people knew skinheads, right-wing radicals, neo-Nazis – and not just from a distance. We were friends with them, we liked some of them, we benefited from their protection. In Manja Präkels' book the chief Nazi might have actually saved the heroine's life. 'The fact that the Nazis were often old friends of ours from school, our brothers, our cousins, made it so difficult to deal with at the time,' says Präkels, 'and that still makes it difficult today.' She also says she sometimes had the feeling someone was holding a protective hand over her. 'Maybe from tender childhood memories of each other. But we didn't have such tenderness for foreigners, for people of colour.'

Nowadays Germans in the east aren't the only ones facing this dilemma; the AfD are gaining ground in the west of the country, too. And if you have to argue with your brother or a friend, then you can't outsource the Nazi problem to Saxony, you've got a German identity crisis on your hands. So, says Präkels, the question is, 'Would we rather sit down with a right-wing extremist we know and pretend everything's normal or call him – and ourselves – into question by standing up for people who are strangers to us?'

I went to Berlin for my community service (in lieu of military service). I started college in Leipzig in 1999. I got lucky and met some good people from the West and the East. If I stuck to the right parts of town, I didn't run into any skinheads. Only once in a while I heard echoes from the past. In the early 2000s a friend of mine found a hole in the rear window of his car: the upstairs neighbours' kid had thrown a vase out of the window. The kid's dad, a skinhead with skinhead chums, didn't feel like paying for the damage and made that clear to my friend. I considered calling my people in Brandenburg, but the Nazi was from Leipzig and wouldn't need to drive two hundred kilometres to strike back with more manpower.

Today, in the small town where I went to school, there are women in headscarves who holler after their sons in Russian to wait for them. There are people serving in bars and cafés whose parents are from Vietnam or Turkey. The friend who once had 'Euthanasie' on his rear window and who I met up with again for this article now says he's friends with 'Kurds, Turks, Russians, Vietnamese'. But he thinks we ought to understand people who'd rather not live alongside so many foreigners. When I ask him if he's one of those people, he says, 'I really don't know.'

I didn't fight, let alone win. I just left.🖌

PERCENTAGE OF VOTES FOR THE AFD

The AfD has gained more support in former East Germany where immigration rates are lower.

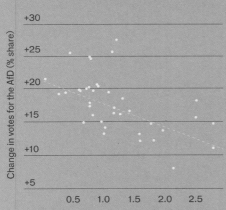

Change in votes for the AfD (% share)

Population increase through immigration (%)

HATE CRIMES

Hate crimes reported in Berlin (2017).

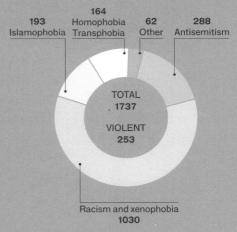

193 Islamophobia

164 Homophobia Transphobia

62 Other

288 Antisemitism

TOTAL
1737

VIOLENT
253

Racism and xenophobia
1030

SOURCE: BERLIN POLICE

VOTED FOR THE AFD

Berlin

- 0–10%
- 10–20%
- 20–30%
- 30–40%

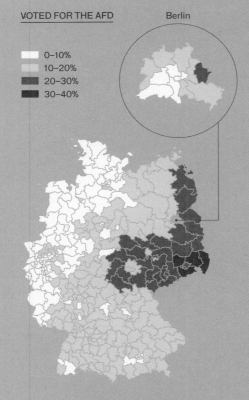

SOURCE: GERMAN FEDERAL RETURNING OFFICER

RIGHT-WING VIOLENCE (2017)

Political violence by the far right per 100,000 inhabitants.

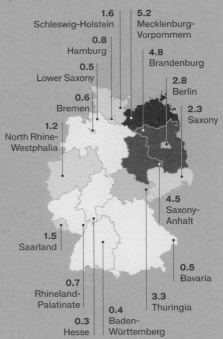

1.6 Schleswig-Holstein

5.2 Mecklenburg-Vorpommern

0.8 Hamburg

4.8 Brandenburg

0.5 Lower Saxony

2.8 Berlin

0.6 Bremen

2.3 Saxony

1.2 North Rhine-Westphalia

4.5 Saxony-Anhalt

1.5 Saarland

0.5 Bavaria

0.7 Rhineland-Palatinate

0.4 Baden-Württemberg

3.3 Thuringia

0.3 Hesse

SOURCE: FEDERAL OFFICE FOR THE PROTECTION OF THE CONSTITUTION, FEDERAL STATISTICAL OFFICE (GERMANY)

Four Square Kilometres of Pure Potential

It was the site of the first Zeppelin flight, the proposed location for megalomaniacal architectural projects conceived during the Nazi era and where the 'raisin bombers' of the Berlin Airlift unloaded their cargos: Tempelhof Airport closed its doors in 2008, and since then the huge green expanse in the heart of the city has become a symbol of young Berliners' desire for liberty.

VINCENZO LATRONICO
Translated by Alan Thawley

Left: 'Flower power': Allmende-Kontor urban garden in Tempelhof Park.

Back when social networking was just making its appearance in a world it would go on to dominate, and the fallout from the economic crisis was fanning the embers that would later spark the drift towards nationalism, for reasons that were not immediately obvious, young people from across the affluent world began to converge on Berlin.

At least, no conscious reason other than theories put forward by observers of the phenomenon: fashion; the urban marketing of the city, with its 'poor-but-sexy' vibe; the very low – then low, then sort of low – cost of living; the myth of Berlin as the moral capital of united Europe, a myth that the subsequent decade would expose as illusory. In hindsight, what seems to me to be the most accurate explanation is also the simplest, namely that nature abhors a void, and the fall of the Wall and reunification had left a lot of empty space.

This is not just a more elegant way of saying it was a question of market forces, of excess supply lowering prices until they intersected with demand; the issue was more fundamental than that. People were looking for free space and the potential that could arise from it. In other words, the void – which obviously means that, strictly speaking, they were looking for something that was not there.

I should say *we* were. I was one of them.

Apartments so huge that most of the space was left unused; empty commercial premises ready to be converted into bars just by ripping the wallpaper and adding a fridge and four mismatched tables; buildings spanning whole city blocks opened up for an exhibition or a squat. Nocturnal wanderings amid deserted warehouses and the skeletons of industrial premises in search of distant parties. I lived in Berlin for five years, from 2009 to 2013, and if I think back to the most vivid images that I keep from that period – the freeze-frames that pop up in your mind when you look back to a given time in your life – they are all images of emptiness.

They are also generic images that could relate to Berlin but equally to Brooklyn or London or Prague or Milan, at least at certain points of their histories. But there is another that seems to me to relate specifically to Berlin during those years: that of Tempelhof, the abandoned airport converted into an illogical park covering almost four square kilometres of flat terrain. It has no trees or pavilions, waterfalls or romantic rocks evoking the raw power of nature. There are not even any paths, just the expansive runways that cut their straight lines across the field. It is the world's largest empty urban space.

Tempelhof Park – its original name was Tempelhofer Freiheit, *Freiheit* meaning 'freedom' – occupies an entire sector to the south of Berlin's urban area proper. Its southern perimeter borders the Stadtring motorway, and its main entrance is six kilometres from the Alexanderplatz tower, which, in a city as large as Berlin, means it almost qualifies as part of the city centre. Were the park circular, it would have a radius of just over a kilometre, an abstract

VINCENZO LATRONICO is a writer and translator based in Germany. He has published several novels and essays (most recently *Un architetto*, 2020, an analysis of the cultural legacy of Albert Speer) in Italian and German and has translated dozens of novels into Italian. He is currently working on new translations of the complete works of George Orwell. He has worked regularly with *Il Sole 24 Ore* and with *Frieze*, and his writings have appeared in *Internazionale*, *Corriere della Sera* and *Frankfurter Allgemeine Zeitung*.

measurement that only serves to highlight the fact that it is twice the size of the Principality of Monaco; to walk from one side of the field to the other as the crow flies would take half an hour at a brisk pace. To put it another way, if you watch the sunset from a balcony overlooking the park on the eastern Neukölln side, the sun disappears into the same empty sky that a sailor might see, the rays reflecting off the asphalt runways like the light bouncing off the ocean, the buildings on the horizon forming a thin, hazy line like a dune or the crest of a distant wave.

The story of Tempelhof is the story of flight. As an expanse of level ground close to the city, it had been used for military drills since the early 19th century, and at the beginning of the 20th it seemed the perfect place for early aeronautical experiments. In 1905 it was the lift-off point for a competition to achieve the longest hot-air balloon flight, won by an incredulous Swiss crew that had time to write their wills in flight before ending up in Norway. Then, in 1909 Count Ferdinand von Zeppelin presented one of his *Luft-Züge*, literally 'air trains', to 300,000 Berliners gathered at Tempelhof decked out in parasols and bowler hats, including Kaiser Wilhelm II.

The Nazis chose it as the site for what was intended to become the airport for the capital city of the world they planned to conquer, as part of their megalomaniacal plan to rename Berlin Welthauptstadt Germania. They drew up plans for what at the time would have been the largest building in Europe, a huge, curved mass which, when viewed from above, would resemble an eagle in flight. The roof would have spanned both terminal and hangars, measuring over a kilometre and a half in length and equipped with viewing stands to accommodate almost 100,000 spectators to watch drills and parades. The

architect, Ernst Sagebiel, had designed it in accordance with *Ruinenwert* theory, whereby plans for official buildings should take into consideration the need for them to eventually leave grandiose ruins worthy of the thousand-year Reich.

A note on Welthauptstadt Germania: the scheme also included plans to erect a gigantic triumphal arch – the largest in the world, naturally. Hitler had said to the architect that it should be clear from afar that it was his. But Albert Speer had his doubts that Berlin's soft soil could support such a massive structure and erected a 12,000-tonne cement cylinder – the *Schwerbelastungskörper*, or 'heavy weight' – on a patch of waste ground near Tempelhof Airport with the aim of recording how far it sank over the years. The Nazis' years were numbered, but sink it certainly did. Yet such a dense and heavy *thing* was deemed difficult to dismantle, unmoveable and dangerous to blow up, so there it remains, an accidental and subtly absurd monument to the capriciousness of dictatorship. In the end, the thousand-year Reich lasted only twelve, and rather than falling into spectacular ruins the terminal was not even completed; after the war the Americans and the police moved in.

But Tempelhof only really entered Berlin's mythology a few years after the war, in 1948, when the Soviet Union blocked all land access to West Berlin in reprisals for the city joining the Marshall Plan. In response, the US, British, Canadian, South African, Australian and New Zealand armed forces organised an air bridge. For over a year it was the entrance point for everything the city needed – almost a thousand flights a day, one landing every three minutes, two million tonnes of *stuff*: food and medicine, fuel, spare parts, raw materials for building and industry, including those needed for the continual repairs to

Above: The airport's former runways are now used by cyclists, skaters and rollerbladers.
Below: The view over Tempelhof's endless expanse of grass. Since closing, the airport has been the city's largest area of green open space.

Above: Relaxing in Tempelhof Park.
Below: Minding the barbecue with the airport's old control tower in the background.

Four Square Kilometres of Pure Potential

the airport itself, which was subject to unprecedented wear and tear.

Some pilots missed the tight landing window and had to return to where they started with their cargo still on board so as not to cause delays. Some pilots died. Some pilots loaded up with supplies of sweet treats that they dropped while flying over the city – the children called them *Rosinenbomber*, 'raisin bombers', but it was often the adults who took advantage, since they were on reduced-calorie rations on the basis that they would find food in the countryside or on the black market anyway.

With the end of the embargo Tempelhof became the main airport for West Berlin, then for the city as a whole, after a period in which it was restricted to military use. But, in spite of its prestige and monumental architecture, it suffered from being small, close to the city centre and unsuitable for modern aircraft, with the result that operations ceased in 2008 on the expectation that its traffic would soon be taken up by Brandenburg Airport, which was under construction at the time. The new hub was due to open in 2011, then in 2015, and only finally became operational in 2020 just as the Covid-19 pandemic was grounding most flights worldwide – the tragic punchline to a joke that had long since ceased to be funny.

I never landed at Tempelhof.

Even now, not having lived in the city for years, I say this with a tinge of embarrassment or perhaps a certain sense of inadequacy, because when I lived in Berlin, having landed at Tempelhof was a badge of credibility of sorts, a hierarchical distinction within an ever-shifting expatriate community. People were proud of their seniority, almost as if it gave them priority rights over the city compared with the waves of new incomers who arrived every summer, flowing out into sublets in

BETTER LATE THAN NEVER?

Flughafen Berlin Brandenburg Willy Brandt, the airport named after the chancellor who set the process of German reunification in motion, was originally due to be opened in 2011, absorbing Schönefeld, the airport on the outskirts of the city, and replacing the beautiful but inefficient Tegel, which was now too close to the city centre. Consequently, Tegel would be transformed from a cause of congestion and noise into a source of stratospheric real-estate profits. Then the construction company went bankrupt, and the opening of the new airport was put back to 2012. But a few days before the ceremony, with the world's media already alerted and the airlines ready to make radical changes to their schedules to help with the move from one destination to another, various issues emerged, including the fact that the fire-safety system had been designed upside down and ninety kilometres of electric cabling failed to comply with regulations. In 2014 a tender process received no applicants, then in 2015 another company folded. In 2016 it emerged that the underground station beneath the terminal also failed to meet regulations. Then in 2017 Air Berlin, the future airport's second most important tenant, went bust. The airport finally opened in October 2020 – nine years late. The Brandt family apparently asked that the statesman's moniker be dropped so as not to tarnish the memory of the great man, but the name stands. Tegel was closed in November 2020, despite the fact that the people of Berlin voted in a referendum for it to remain open after the completion of Brandenburg, being more convenient and closer to the centre.

Wedding and Neukölln and then draining away when faced with their first winter or the expiry of their tourist visas. So, to distinguish themselves, the old guard would brandish their rental agreements made out in Deutschmarks, their memories of the old squats or air tickets marked for arrival at THF. To those who only know today's park, full of kiteboarders and families having barbecues, the days when that colossal ruin was a working airport must seem remote, part of that same time when, to call your boyfriend, you had to negotiate with his dad on the landline and you had to hide from velociraptors at night.

The abandoned airfield was converted into a park in 2010, and the following year, thanks to the centrifugal force of rising property prices, I moved to an apartment one street away from the side entrance. The first time I visited I just ended up there, following a friend who was showing me around the jogging routes of my new locale. I would meet Assaf every morning at seven at the foot of a lesser control tower. Sometimes the sun had already long been up, the sky clear but with the rarefied air of northern Europe, like crystal ready to shatter. Sometimes it was pitch black with half a metre of snow on the ground. We would walk briskly to the start of the runway and carry on for a kilometre and a half to the Nazis' colossal terminal, then back around the perimeter. More or less halfway we would pass by what must have been a confectionery factory, announcing its presence with irresistible wafts of chocolate and cream. Over the forty-five or fifty minutes we ran we almost never came into contact with another soul in that park the size of a city state, but in winter some runners fixed flashing safety lights to their tops, and from a distance we worked out their routes by following their pulsing red wakes as if on a sonar screen.

Running brought organisation and therefore a purpose to the space, but when I found myself returning to Tempelhof on other occasions I was always struck by the anarchy, the blatant illogicality of that flat, treeless park too vast to be tied down to a single function. Over the years shared gardens and a barbecue area have sprung up, along with proper toilets and even a reserve for the breeding of certain species of bird, and yet any kind of subdivision merely chips at the edges, barely touching them, so that what is set aside for a specific purpose serves only to make the centre given over to the runways and fallow land more absurd by contrast.

The question of what to do with four square kilometres of useless space in one of Europe's largest cities might seem paradoxical. It might also seem immoral, given the catastrophic housing situation in Berlin caused by population growth, the explosion of short-term tourist lets and the massive influx of speculative capital – in 2017 alone real-estate prices rose by 20 per cent. This problem does not only affect the penniless artists, students, lazy expats, hippies, people on the margins of society and runaways who have determined the capital's identity over the past two or three decades but also – and much more seriously – an ever-growing number of families and workers. Recently a movement demanding the compulsory purchase and renationalisation of the public housing sold off for a pittance after reunification has been gathering support: over half a million apartments, almost two hundred thousand of which are in the hands of just three companies. By way of comparison, two hundred thousand apartments is roughly equal to the number of homes in the US city of Atlanta.

At the very point at which I finished writing the previous sentence I saw on

A couple takes a break in Tempelhof Park's Allmende-Kontor urban garden.

Twitter that Berlin's Senate (the German capital has the status of a city state) had voted to freeze all rents in the city for five years. This is a relief but a little like the relief felt by a hero trapped by an evil genius in a room when the rising water stops at their chin: the fact remains that they are still trapped.

This is why the city authorities called a referendum in 2014 to consider the possibility of reallocating around a fifth of the park for housing, with plans to build five thousand apartments, a proportion of them earmarked for social housing. The city – the same city that has now collected 300,000 signatures in favour of compulsory purchases – voted no.

The results of the referendum were analysed extensively, and a number of different conclusions were reached. Perhaps Berliners did not have faith in the effectiveness of the social aspect of the project, considering how tolerant of private speculation the authorities had been in previous years. Or perhaps they did have faith but didn't feel it made up for the transformation of the best parts of the park into yet another luxury enclave. Perhaps they found the alternative plans more convincing – one of them, which went viral, involved the creation of a mountain over a kilometre high in the park; to be known as *Berg*, 'mountain', it would have become a natural oasis but also a ski resort for the people of Berlin – or perhaps they just wanted to hold on to the empty space.

The fact remains that the empty space is still there and is used for real-life role-play games – dozens, sometimes hundreds, of people who arrange to meet up on a snowy morning to dress up as crusaders and do battle with plastic swords – but also for picnics, running, meditation, sleeping and enjoying what could almost be a sunset over the ocean. It has hosted concerts and conferences. Germany's largest refugee camp was set up there.

There is always something unsatisfactory and superficial to the logic by which a landmark becomes a symbol of a city. The process is driven more by chance and marketing concerns than a search for meaning. From this perspective, in the family that includes the Colosseum, the Eiffel Tower, Tower Bridge, Sydney Opera House and the Golden Gate Bridge, the Brandenburg Gate has a profound, double historical value in its favour. Built to represent peace in the 18th century, almost three centuries later it became the symbolic centre of the reunification of a city torn apart by the Cold War and as such represents the starting point of today's Berlin. But, to my mind, the city's identity since then is better reflected by a place with a history ranging from such grandiose events as the flight of the Zeppelin to terrible periods such as the Nazi dictatorship and moving episodes like the planes dropping sweets over the city, a welcoming, disorganised place, too chaotic for rules to be imposed on those who decide to take up residence for an hour, a month or a decade. A reserve of space so vast that it frustrates anyone trying to corral it to a specific purpose and therefore destined to stay as it is, open and illogical, four square kilometres of pure potential.

Or perhaps not. Even though the law that followed the referendum prevents construction, every so often a new building project for the former airport pops up. Driven out by the ever-rising cost of living, Assaf returned to Israel and I moved to the countryside in Mecklenburg-Vorpommern. To the incredulous Berliners who ask me why, I reply that it is only two hours north and is among Europe's least densely populated regions. I was twenty-three when I arrived in Berlin; I am now thirty-six. 🖋

Old airport signage.

Wherever you go in Berlin it seems you stumble upon a new Vietnamese restaurant. This is more than a simple case of supply meeting an increased demand: the city's large and diverse Vietnamese community is the result of shared experiences in the histories of Germany and Vietnam, two countries divided by conflict and later reunified.

The entrance to the Dong Xuan Vietnamese shopping centre in the Lichtenberg district of Berlin.

Berlin's Little Vietnam

ALISA ANH KOTMAIR

EAST–WEST MEETS NORTH–SOUTH

Berlin's population of some 3.77 million includes people from all over the world, yet one ethnic group in particular stands out: the Vietnamese. Vietnamese restaurants seem to be opening up everywhere around the city, and their popularity signals that there is room for more. Germans love their flowers, and in nearly every U-Bahn or S-Bahn station you can find a Vietnamese-run flower stand. And whereas many corner groceries and late-night shops in the western part of the city are run by Turkish or Arab immigrants, it is Vietnamese corner shops that dominate the eastern part of the city. This phenomenon can be traced back to the unique relationship between Vietnam and Germany and their recent histories of division and reunification. While Germany and its capital city Berlin were divided into East and West, into communist and capitalist, Vietnam was divided into North and South, also along similar ideological lines. These parallels are reflected in the city's Vietnamese population.

A BRIEF HISTORY OF MIGRATION

The first Vietnamese migrants came to Germany while both countries were still divided. Students from the former Republic of South Vietnam came to West Germany to study in the 1960s; because of the Vietnam War most of them remained in Germany and went on to work in highly skilled jobs. In East Germany, the first Vietnamese came in the mid-1950s from the former Democratic Republic of Vietnam in the north – a group of children aged ten to fourteen, who returned to Vietnam after high school. An estimated fifty thousand university students and trainees from northern Vietnam were also sent in the 1960s and 1970s. While many of them returned to Vietnam, a number of them found ways to remain or to return to Germany through work opportunities.

In the aftermath of the Vietnam War until the opening up of the country in the early 1990s, an estimated two million Vietnamese fled the country, around 800,000 of them by boat. West Germany took in nearly forty thousand 'boat people' from around the late 1970s to the mid-1980s, settling many of them in Lower Saxony, Bavaria and West Berlin. They were given permits to remain and work, language courses, access to education and vocational training and financial and social support to aid their integration into society.

On the other side of Germany, the GDR strengthened its post-Vietnam War relationship with the new Socialist Republic of Vietnam. In much the same way as 'guest workers' were recruited to the FRG between the 1950s and 1970s (from Italy, Spain, Greece, Morocco, Portugal, Tunisia, Yugoslavia and Turkey), the GDR started a similar programme in the 1960s to recruit temporary 'contract workers' from fellow socialist and communist countries. These included Poland, Hungary, North Korea, Angola, Mozambique, Cuba and, from the 1980s onwards, Vietnam. Around seventy thousand Vietnamese came to

ALISA ANH KOTMAIR is a Vietnamese-American artist, writer, editor and translator. Based in Berlin for more than twenty years, she has observed and addressed issues concerning the visibility and representation of the Vietnamese diaspora through the performing and visual arts and written work. Her short film about the Vietnamese-German experience, *Sunday Menu*, directed under the pseudonym Liesl Nguyen, premiered at the 2011 Berlinale. She contributed to the book *Asiatische Deutsche: Vietnamesische Diaspora and Beyond* (2nd edition, 2021).

'The cliché of the smiling Asian, peaceful, obedient and acquiescent, contributes to the non-threatening image ascribed to the Vietnamese as a model minority whose core values are compatible with those of the German majority.'

the GDR between 1980 and 1989 this way, comprising around two-thirds of the contract workers in East Germany, many of them in East Berlin. Contract workers in the GDR were housed in same-sex dormitories and contact with East Germans outside of work was discouraged; women who became pregnant were forced to have an abortion or be deported. Integration was not the aim; they were expected to stay a few years and then return to their native country.

When the Berlin Wall fell in 1989 the contract workers found themselves in a legal grey zone, unsure if they could remain in reunified Germany. As visible foreigners, Vietnamese were increasingly targeted in xenophobic incidents. Nevertheless, around half of the Vietnamese former contract workers decided to try their luck in Germany. Most became self-employed, opening up food stands or small restaurants, clothing stalls at open markets, flower shops, corner groceries, tailor's shops or nail salons. Through their perseverance, these independent, service-sector businesses have helped to shape the German landscape over the years, particularly in Berlin.

Throughout the 1990s and into the new millennium many more Vietnamese have come to Germany through family reunification programmes from former Eastern bloc states, to study or to do business. Inner migration has occurred as Vietnamese, like Germans, have moved from poorer areas in the east to more prosperous cities – like the capital city Berlin. Of an estimated 170,000 people with Vietnamese roots living in Germany today, more than half of them have a German passport. Around twenty-six thousand of them live in Berlin, with another estimated ten to twenty thousand living in the capital city unofficially.

In the 1990s the Vietnamese, particularly in eastern Germany, were stigmatised as criminals because of those who, unable to find work or without legal status, turned to the sale of untaxed cigarettes. This activity came to be dominated by Vietnamese gangs, and their violence drew widespread media attention. While gang activity continues, extending into other European countries with human trafficking linked to prostitution, child labour and illegal drugs, it tends to go under the radar as it does not affect Germans directly. Other ethnic minorities are much more present in the media, which accuses them of failing to integrate into German society, organising into clan structures and abusing the social-welfare system.

In stark contrast, the children of Vietnamese former contract workers and refugees, born and/or raised in Germany, have been hailed as the 'Vietnamese wonder' for their educational success, even surpassing Germans in terms of class rankings, examination scores and university admissions. The cliché of the smiling Asian, peaceful, obedient and acquiescent, contributes to the non-threatening image

VIETNAMESE 'BOAT PEOPLE' AND WEST GERMAN HUMANITARIAN AID

In 1978 the city of Hanover in Lower Saxony, West Germany (FRG), welcomed the first thousand Vietnamese 'boat people' – refugees who had fled Vietnam by boat in the aftermath of the war – becoming the first group of refugees to come to the FRG from outside Europe. West Germany went on to take in nearly forty thousand in total, significantly fewer than the USA, Australia and France but enough to spark a fierce debate. Some West German politicians voiced their fear of Germany becoming a 'country of immigration', while others did not want to encourage flight from Vietnam as a newly united country – but many did show their support. In 1980 the new category of 'humanitarian refugee' was created, which allowed Vietnamese refugees to bypass the otherwise lengthy process of asylum and secure residence and work permits more quickly. They also received extensive support to assist their integration in society, such as language courses, vocational training and advisory services. Media coverage of Vietnam and humanitarian efforts helped to sensitise the German public to their plight. Hearing about the numbers of people stranded in overcrowded boats as they attempted to flee, exposed to the elements and under threat of attack by pirates, one West German couple, Christel and Rupert Neudeck, founded a charitable organisation to assist them. Funded by donations, their ship *Cap Anamur* took teams of volunteer technicians, doctors and nurses to rescue some ten thousand Vietnamese in the South China Sea between 1979 and 1986.

THE PASSENGER   Alisa Anh Kotmair

ascribed to the Vietnamese as a model minority whose core values are compatible with those of the German majority.

What better migrants then, to look after our loved ones: once again, Germany is actively recruiting Vietnamese to the country. To compensate for the chronic shortage in professional caregivers – a low-paid sector – for Germany's large ageing population, a programme has been established to train nurses from Vietnam to provide geriatric care in Germany.

BERLIN'S LITTLE HANOI

While Vietnamese refugees who came to West Berlin tended to be more integrated into German society, the many former contract workers in the East – generally less integrated and often with poorer German-language skills – mostly settled in the same neighbourhoods, where they nurtured support networks. The largest concentration of Vietnamese in Berlin is in the eastern district of Lichtenberg; there is even a state-run bilingual German-Vietnamese kindergarten and a high school with a strong focus on supporting the district's many students with Vietnamese roots. This is also home to the Dong Xuan Center, an epicentre of Vietnamese life in Berlin, said to be the second largest Asian market in all of Europe.

Named after the large historic market in Hanoi, it was founded by Nguyen Van Hien, who came to Germany as a thirty-year-old contract worker from northern Vietnam in 1988. After German reunification he opened his first wholesale market in Leipzig in 1996, then in 2003 acquired a former industrial complex in Berlin. Over the years the Dong Xuan Center has grown from one to eight halls, each nearly two hundred metres long – conscientiously covered in solar panels – and with a total area of approximately 165,000 square metres. Around

two thousand people earn their livelihoods here, from Vietnam, China, India, Pakistan, Poland and Turkey. Here you can find wholesale suppliers of cut flowers, textiles, plastic goods and electronics, food, beauty-salon equipment, as well as Asian-food grocery stores, Vietnamese restaurants, karaoke, hair salons and tattoo parlours. Services catering to the Vietnamese community include translation and travel agencies, lawyers and tax advisors as well as driving schools. And there are community events, too, celebrating Vietnamese new year or hosting association gatherings, musical concerts and more.

Nguyen Van Hien continues to pursue his vision: to establish a true Vietnamese quarter in the area, with a cultural centre, pagoda, hotel, apartment buildings and even a noodle factory – so that Asian noodles don't have to be imported but can proudly carry the seal 'made in Germany'.

CHINATOWN OF WEST BERLIN

While the east of the city has 'Little Hanoi', Kantstrasse has long been informally known as the Chinatown of West Berlin or, for the more politically correct, 'Little Asia'. Chinese students started coming to Berlin in the late 1800s to study at nearby universities, and the city's first Chinese restaurant opened in Kantstrasse in 1923, with more following, until the violence and destruction of the Second World War. Especially in post-reunification Berlin, the street has drawn a host of Asian-themed shops and restaurants. Ethnic markers are blurred here: there are Vietnamese selling sushi and burgers and Chinese selling ramen. The German cake shop has Thai and Korean employees, while the bonsai store is run by an American. Meanwhile, young people of all nationalities can be seen sitting at the Arab-run shisha bar. Complementing the Cantonese, Taiwanese,

'Ethnic markers are blurred here: there are Vietnamese selling sushi and burgers and Chinese selling ramen. The German cake shop has Thai and Korean employees, while the bonsai store is run by an American.'

Thai, Japanese, Korean and Vietnamese speciality restaurants are tasty fusions. The latter not only cater to growing German tastes for all things Asian but also reflect younger generations of entrepreneurs expressing their transcultural identities and perspectives in their business ventures.

FROM REFUGEE TO CELEBRATED CHEF

No fewer than five restaurants on Kant-strasse are the brainchild of The Duc Ngo, a Vietnamese-Chinese-German chef who has helped to shape the culinary landscape in Berlin.

Born in 1974, Ngo and his family fled Hanoi in the face of growing discrimination as a Chinese-Vietnamese family. Arriving by boat to a refugee camp in Hong Kong, they were among the first Vietnamese refugees to be settled in West Berlin in 1979.

Ngo was drawn to cooking at an early age, and, while still a student of Japanology at a local university, he apprenticed himself to one of West Berlin's first sushi bars. After training in various restaurants and gaining inspiration abroad, Ngo, together with his cousin and his brother, opened Kuchi in Kantstrasse in 1999, then a second Kuchi in the trendy former East Berlin neighbour-hood of Mitte in 2001. The novel concept – an upmarket Asian-fusion restaurant with sushi but also noodles and meat dishes presented in a hip, cosmopolitan decor – quickly attracted Berlin scenesters and celebrity guests. This sparked a wave of Vietnamese-run restaurants to embrace sushi-Vietnamese fusion as a recipe for success.

Several years and gourmet restau-rant experiences later, Ngo returned to Kantstrasse in 2016, launching four restaurants near the original Kuchi in the space of just a few years. With numerous family members involved in operations, one might speak of a dynasty (or clan), albeit one well integrated into German culture and catering to, even advancing, its tastes. At Madame Ngo patrons are greeted with the sight and smells of huge vats of bubbling broth for traditional Vietnamese chicken and beef pho soup. French dishes and the brasserie-like interior are a nod to the influence of French colonialism on Vietnamese cuisine. According to Ngo, it's a 'homage to my parents, my family, and the country and the city of Hanoi where I was born'. Just across the street is 893 Ryotei with Japanese-Peruvian fusion cuisine, the upmarket fish restaurant, Funky Fisch, and NgoKimPak, billed as a 'fun Asian eatery'. Each restaurant has a distinct visual identity developed by Ngo's long-time collaborator, Korean designer Hyunjung Kim.

'I cook fusion cuisine because I am myself a fusion,' Ngo has said. In his restaurants, he expresses the fluid nature of his identity shaped by his ethnic heritage, upbringing and evolving personal tastes. An appear-ance on the German cooking show *Kitchen Impossible* gave Ngo the opportunity not only to introduce Vietnamese pho to a nationwide television audience but also to prove his culinary versatility and expertise in preparing both traditional Austrian and American cuisine.

COFFEE – THE CROP THAT BROUGHT TWO NATIONS TOGETHER

In 1975 a frost decimated the coffee harvest in Brazil, the world's largest coffee producer, triggering an enormous hike in global coffee prices. For the GDR this meant quadrupling the amount of hard currency it needed to import coffee, which was already a scarce commodity in the country. Although prices stabilised a few years later, the GDR sought alternative coffee sources through barter with socialist partners. In short-lived deals with Ethiopia and Angola, for instance, it traded weapons and heavy equipment for the crop. With Laos and Vietnam, however, it tried to establish a more sustainable solution, and throughout the 1980s the GDR helped to revive the coffee industry in both countries, which had been established by French colonials in the early 20th century. The GDR supplied the countries with technology, materials and training, and in Vietnam it also built massive infrastructure – housing, hospitals, stores, even a hydroelectric-power plant – for thousands of people who were relocated to the central highlands to tend new Robusta coffee plantations. In exchange the GDR would receive around half of both countries' annual coffee harvests starting in the mid-1980s. Unfortunately the GDR was unable to reap much reward for its efforts, thanks to the fall of the Berlin Wall in 1989. However, its significant investments helped Vietnam to become the world's second largest coffee producer, and today Germany is the second biggest importer, after the USA, of Vietnamese green coffee beans.

For Ngo, notions of authenticity are less important than passion and quality. 'Cooks who love a certain type of food will dedicate themselves to making it as good as possible, often even better than natives who grow up with it, because they have to make an extra effort to prove themselves,' he notes. 'I try to learn as much as possible about a cuisine, and then give it my own twist. You don't want to exploit the culture but approach it with respect.'

Above: German-Vietnamese couple Sascha Wölck and Hang Hoang with their children May and Kim.

IN SEARCH OF THE AUTHENTIC
Whereas Vietnamese in Berlin were previously hesitant to assert their culture through cuisine, masking their cultural identity by selling Chinese, Thai or Japanese food, they are now asserting their cultural identity by selling distinctly Vietnamese food. From a marketing perspective, the appeal of the authentic is paying off.

A pioneer in this respect is Dat Vuong, who was the first to open an openly Vietnamese bistro in Mitte in 1999 and was immediately embraced by the scene. He named the restaurant Monsieur Vuong after his father, with whom he left Saigon at the age of twelve, arriving in West Germany in 1987 to join his mother and two siblings who had fled the communist regime several years earlier.

Si An Truong, who also came from Saigon with his family to West Germany in the 1980s, can be credited with intensifying the Vietnam experience in Berlin by pairing Vietnamese food with iconic interiors. These include Chén Chè, the decor of which evokes the romance of a tea house

FOREIGNERS IN BERLIN

Regions and countries of origin (as at 30 June 2020).

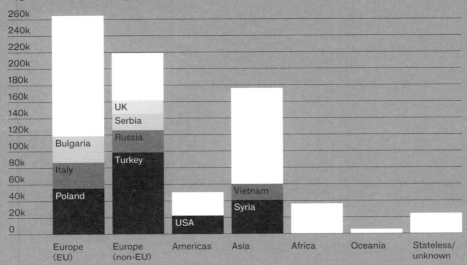

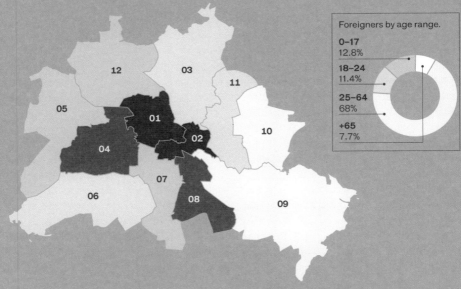

% of foreigners	
0–9%	
10–14%	
15–19%	
20–24%	
+25%	

01. Mitte
02. Friedrichshain-Kreuzberg
03. Pankow
04. Charlottenburg-Wilmersdorf
05. Spandau
06. Steglitz-Zehlendorf

07. Tempelhof-Schöneberg
08. Neukölln
09. Treptow-Köpenick
10. Marzahn-Hellersdorf
11. Lichtenberg
12. Reinickendorf

SOURCE: BERLIN-BRANDENBURG OFFICE OF STATISTICS

'It is too easily forgotten that a dormitory for Vietnamese refugees was set on fire by right-wing radicals in Hamburg in the 1980s; two people died. The incident was used by politicians as an excuse to tighten immigration law in West Germany.'

in French Indochina, and Đistrict Một, a brash celebration of the plastic, makeshift aesthetic of Saigon street food.

Meanwhile, younger generations are carving out their own niches in the culinary landscape. Duc Nguyen and Hong Dao bring together Vietnamese and Berlin coffee culture with Quà Phê and Maison Han. Nguyen's Han Coffee Roasters sources coffee directly from Vietnam. Their interiors blend traditional Vietnamese and minimalist elements for a cool, casual vibe that speaks to the clientele of millennial global nomads gathered in Berlin. Nguyen's family is from the south of Vietnam and came as refugees to West Berlin, while Dao is from the north. Her mother came as a contract worker and then brought the rest of her family in the late 1990s to live in the eastern part of Berlin. As such, the couple represents a new generation that transcends former political divides between north and south, east and west.

Instead of romantic images of traditional Vietnam, the team of Ulteamate Berlin aims to infuse the Berlin scene with a contemporary East Asian trend. Inspired by the success of smart bubble-tea cafés in Hanoi, Ngoc Hoang decided to launch her own business in Berlin. Hoang and her business partner Maikel Nguyen, both in their twenties, were born in reunified Germany to parents who came to the GDR as contract workers. 'I always knew I wanted to be my own boss,' says Hoang. 'Even though our parents would love for us

to have secure jobs, they themselves were forced to be self-employed in Germany, and we learned from their example,' she explains. Unlike her parents, Hoang did not get vocational training in Germany; she went to Vietnam for several months of bubble-tea training and brought her expertise back to Germany in a case of reverse knowledge transfer.

SPEAKING FOR THE SILENT

While food is the most obvious way in which Berlin's Vietnamese community is finally making itself seen, there are many others drawing awareness to the diverse Vietnamese population. Mai-Phuong Kollath, for example, has dedicated much of her four decades in the country to building bridges between the Vietnamese and Germans as a diversity coach and consultant.

She knows the subject well, having negotiated cultural differences herself many times over to carve out her own destiny in Germany. Arriving in the GDR in 1981 as a seventeen-year-old from Hanoi, she expected to gain skills in the hotel business but was instead thrust into a simple cafeteria kitchen job. She defied the rules by falling in love with a German and hiding her pregnancy until it was too late for her to be deported. After German reunification she worked during the day in a childcare centre and evenings at a small Vietnamese food stand, which she ran with her husband to make ends meet. Among her customers were right-wing youths

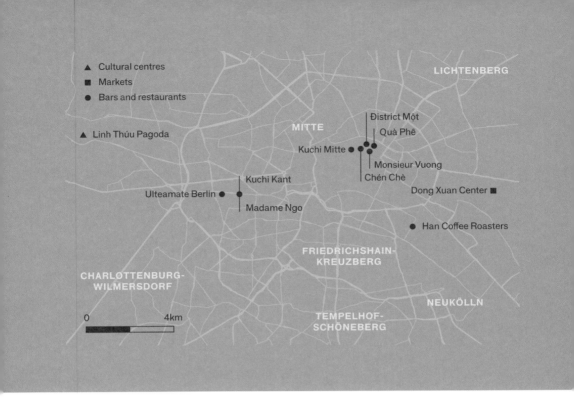

Above: A map of the Vietnamese locations mentioned in this article.

whose pastime included making xenophobic remarks about Vietnamese former contract workers.

In the face of anti-immigrant sentiments, the stigma of the cigarette mafia and fear of losing their livelihoods and residency status, many Vietnamese in eastern Germany sought to avoid confrontation with Germans, often downplaying their ethnicity outside of familiar circles. This, combined with a lack of German-language skills, underscored their reputation as quiet, unproblematic minorities. Kollath,

on the other hand, decided to retaliate against the discrimination she experienced by retraining as a social educator and intercultural trainer. After years of advocating for the Vietnamese community in Rostock she moved to Berlin in 2011. 'In Rostock I felt quite alone in my work. In Berlin I have met so many more people, especially from the one-and-a-half and second generations, who are much more outspoken,' she says. These include a growing number of academics, journalists and artists from the Vietnamese diaspora, drawn to Berlin as a cosmopolitan, affordable city. These global-minded citizens can enjoy a hybrid identity that does not necessarily register on any census.

In Berlin, Kollath has also been able to reach a wider and more diverse audience through collaborations in theatre and

Right: The Duc Ngo, the noted Vietnamese chef and owner of a number of restaurants in Berlin, including NgoKimPak in Charlottenburg, which also features in the photograph on page 87.

film, to share her own story of migration and the wider history of Vietnamese in Germany. For too long the Vietnamese have been overlooked as an 'invisible minority' in German society. Seen as well integrated and hard working, they are not perceived as a threat to the social-welfare system, nor do they voice complaints in the face of discrimination, and they are barely represented in politics or the mass media. It is too easily forgotten that a dormitory for Vietnamese refugees was set on fire by right-wing radicals in Hamburg in the 1980s; two people died. The incident was used by politicians as an excuse to tighten immigration law in West Germany. Or that in 1992 in the former East German suburb of Rostock-Lichtenhagen, an apartment building where Vietnamese lived was set on fire by hooligans as a horde of Germans stood around cheering for days, with no support provided afterwards to the Vietnamese victims by the local authorities.

Kollath recalls how, long ago, her mother tried to convince her not to stay in Germany because of its horrific role in the Second World War. As a young person she laughed off her mother's concerns, but today Kollath is more pensive. 'Nowadays you can see so many parallels with the past, with the refugees and with people acting more openly racist. Sometimes I am worried that things could shift quickly in the wrong direction.'

HYBRID IDENTITIES

The complexities and nuances of the Vietnamese–German relationship are confronted by Sascha and Hang on a daily basis as a young binational family. Hang came to Berlin to study German and cultural studies, while Sascha moved to Berlin from Kiel to study Southeast Asian studies and wrote his PhD on Vietnam. Both are supporting the Vietnamese community through their work: while Hang works as a job coach, Sascha deals with cultural and generational gaps between traditionally minded Vietnamese parents and their German-assimilated children. 'There is a lot to do in cases where parents and child have no common language,' says Sascha, who, like his wife, is fluent in both Vietnamese and German. This is a situation they are consciously trying to avoid in raising their two children bilingually in the dynamic, multicultural neighbourhood of Neukölln. Although Hang misses the strong family ties she had in Vietnam, she, like many others who live in Berlin, appreciates the city for its sense of freedom and space, the environmental awareness and the robust social system, especially in terms of education and healthcare; in Vietnam those things are hard to come by or come at a high cost.

So, if not Vietnam then Berlin – with its diverse, vibrant and growing Vietnamese community – might just be the next best place to be. 🐦

Berlin Suite

Spring 1991: the great Dutch writer and
traveller Cees Nooteboom, who had
witnessed the fall of the Wall when he lived
in Berlin between 1989 to 1990, returned
to the reunified city for the first time.
Euphoria had given way to anxiety, and an
invisible wall of recrimination and suspicion
still divided the city, while the absence of
certainty and the weight of unanswered
questions cast their shadow over all.

Cees Nooteboom

Translated by Laura Watkinson

95

The final photograph in Part I of my book *Roads to Berlin* (MacLehose, 2012) shows the Belvedere in the gardens of Schloss Sanssouci in Potsdam, and the last sentence of that section ended with the words: 'and, when I return, everything will be different, yet still the same, and changed forever'. It was in itself not a difficult prediction to make. The Wall would be gone, but the familiar buildings would still remain, and the two parts of the city would, I believed, slowly move towards each other along with the people who lived there. Old newspapers would disappear and new ones would take their place, West Berlin would become busier and busier, and in the East the signs of capitalism would start making gradual inroads. I recently went back to visit the Belvedere. It was no longer the open, wounded ruin it had been since the war, dismantled, violated, weeds among the pillars. Its decay was wrapped up like one of Christo's buildings, the desecration invisible. The signs of war will disappear from this building; it will no longer serve as a memento. On the contrary, if it ever resurfaces from beneath those black rags it will gleam, a model of classical architectural style, a showpiece. Yet it will also look a little dead, like an actress with a facelift.

What kind of city had I returned to? I still did not know. This was, in fact, a double return: the first in February, the second in April. In the intervening period the doubt had intensified; it was becoming

CEES NOOTEBOOM is a Dutch novelist, poet, essayist and travel writer. Described by *The New York Times* as 'an impressive and inimitable voice among contemporary writers', his work has been translated into more than thirty languages and has garnered numerous literary awards, being compared with Borges, Calvino and Nabokov. Born in The Hague, his first novel, *Philip and the Others*, was published in 1954 when he was only twenty-one, and he went on to achieve international success with novels such as *Rituals* (1980) and *The Following Story* (1991). He experienced the fall of the Berlin Wall first hand, recounting it in his Berlin diaries (published in English as *Roads to Berlin: Detours and Riddles in the Lands and History of Germany*, MacLehose Press, 2012), from which this essay is extracted.

increasingly difficult to say anything about the situation. I myself remained more or less the same, even though no one steps in the same river twice. The setting was also the same: same city, same house, same wooden lion on the handrail in the dark hallway, same smell of tobacco and German food in the stairwell. My Chilean friend had taken some of his books and paintings away to the other side of the earth, but there was still enough Spanish there to keep a reader occupied for a year, and the strange furniture of exile also remained. It snowed on my first return, and the chestnut tree in the courtyard still reached close to my windows, and I could see how cold the tree felt. The neighbours with the children in the flat opposite had disappeared and the new ones were invisible. The old woman beneath me, who was the oldest resident and had known the house before the war ('you simply can't imagine what the bombings were like'), had become increasingly confused over the past few months, and then she had died. I wondered if anyone in the world still thought about her sometimes. Big cities allow people to disappear without a trace, but I can still picture her big shoes, her stiff gait, her closed expression. But no one ever mentioned her. A company with the word 'Europe' in its name had moved in on her floor. The people I sometimes saw coming out of there looked as though they had stepped straight out of an advertisement.

I went on scouting expeditions in the snow. I remember one time encountering a surviving piece of Wall with metal rods sticking out of it, a dead, snow-covered passageway, the rods like grasping, black tentacles, but nothing happened. I stood there on that narrow piece of land that would soon be ordinary again, part of a much larger piece of land, with no more than traces, imprints of the two missing walls in the soil, and I realised that there was nothing to say. Any thoughts about that concrete memory had been thought to death; like the Wall itself, they had met their end. It felt much stranger in those places where the Wall no longer was, at Checkpoint Charlie, for instance. But you could no longer say 'at

Checkpoint Charlie' either, because now it existed only in photographs. Describing a place in terms of what is no longer there can be difficult. The Wall that is no longer there exists in duplicate, because you have to imagine it in the place where it once actually was. Or maybe not, but it happens automatically. You cannot walk through a wound unharmed, and that wound is everywhere. As are the scars. Many of the checkpoint buildings are still standing, empty, pointless. They have to go, or someone needs to find a use for them. The currency exchange office at Invalidenstrasse has become a Beate Uhse sex shop, which is sure to go down well. Slowly the big clean-up will begin, but that is outside, in the city. The inner clean-up will have to wait for people who have not yet been born, for the new inhabitants or for the unthinking, but there are few of those. It seems as though everyone has the Wall in their mind; sooner or later it comes up in every conversation. Are people becoming used to it? Not really. You can now hop on to the S-Bahn to the East without having to get off at Bahnhof Friedrichstrasse; you just carry on through. The train windows sketch the city for you: the gap where the Wall once stood, the drabness, the Stalinist architecture, the other. No, you cannot get used to that, and you cannot blow it up either; it is going to remain intact. Soon rents for the unpainted houses will rise, and growing numbers of unemployed people will be living in those colourless buildings. And that, too, is a Wall of a kind.

And what about the West, where the privileged people live? They are unhappy, sometimes even malicious; I will come back to them later. And they keep themselves to themselves. In fact, it feels as though, after the initial euphoria, the Wall has returned. If you have no business being in the other part, East or West, you stay at home. Too expensive for one, too shabby for the other: 'The people in the East have a sergeant-major mentality. There's no talking to them.' 'The people in the West are arrogant. They want to colonise us.' 'They put up with that system for forty years. What does that say about them? One person in six was a member of the

Stasi. Can you imagine that mentality? That's all we need!' 'Money, money, money, it's all those *Wessis* think about. They think we're all beggars. They were just lucky. Coming over here for a nice little tour in their great big Mercedes, seeing if they can find an old house of theirs still standing.'

'Don't you think it's all changed?' friends ask me. You don't want to say so, but you think that perhaps they are the ones who have changed; you are amazed at their bitterness. They go on and on about rising crime rates, but I come from a city with its own problems, so I am not impressed. The long lines of Poles outside the cheap supermarkets and electronics shops on Kantstrasse that they were complaining about so much last year have not returned, in spite of the new visa freedom. Most of the Trabants are staying in their dens or their owners have bought Western cars. The petrol is a better quality, so the stench has gone. The West of the city is once again its former, park-like self. House prices are rising daily, and in every respect this is the most peaceful metropolis I know; even the May Day riots were less violent this year than tradition dictates. Anything else? Just people living and waiting. They are waiting for better roads and a decision about whether Berlin will be the capital city, waiting for a balanced budget and for new buildings on Potsdamer Platz (see 'The Greatest Show in Town' on page 13), for the Mielke trial and for new immigrants, for work and for revelations, for investments and bankruptcies. The entire city is sitting in the waiting room of history, and while everything that happens here is very real, there is still a sense of unreality about the streets and squares, as though this world might not be real, as though something completely different might yet happen and nobody knows what, but whatever it is it will have something to do with the idea of history. This city cannot escape history, and perhaps that is the issue here or one of the issues.

History should be something that has already happened not something that is happening now. Anyone who believes he is making history cannot keep his mind focused on reality, but a city that is saturated with signs of the past, with planned statues and chance bullet holes, with damaged columns alongside intact ones, a city that reads like one large memory in stone, a city that is reminded every day of its role from before and even before that, is not free to move in the present. History is invisible because it happens so slowly; only very rarely does it allow itself to be hurried along. One such moment was that day in November 1989, but the consequences of that day are moving with the slow deliberation of a chess move, and the city's inhabitants are the people who will have to make the next move, and they will also have to wait for the results – and there is more evidence of waiting than doing. They while away their time in the waiting room by talking, complaining, arguing, blaming, investigating, remembering, condemning, asking. The pages in this history book are as heavy as the lead in Kiefer's books: you can turn over only one page a year at most.

But do you really think, you peculiar Outsider, that the Berliners you can see sitting in the weak spring sunshine on a bench behind Schloss Charlottenburg, or their distant fellow citizens who are looking with a mixture of embarrassment and bewilderment at the pale and pimply faces of the Hare Krishnas bouncing up and down on Alexanderplatz in the East, are that bothered about the idea of history?

'*Jein*,' I would have to answer, like a true Berliner: both *ja* and *nein*, because how can you not think about history at such a time? Historic: the word pops out of politicians' mouths on a regular basis ('If we miss out on this historic opportunity ...') and strides through the editorials and television commentaries. Monuments still testify to history: the days of your own lifetime can turn to stone and take the form of a ruin, a half-demolished Wall, a façade full of bullet holes or a colossal statue of a grieving mother with a fallen son in her arms. And there is another way in which almost everyone here is affected by history – even the youngest citizens of the former GDR were members of the FDJ (Freie Deutsche Jugend, Free German Youth). If you go further back in time you encounter all kinds of different combinations: people who, under Hitler, were on the wrong side and after him were nothing, people who were on the wrong side twice, people who were heroes during the Nazi era and then joined the Stasi, and all shades in between, from fanaticism to indifference. You meet them and you do not know who they were; they carry their invisible pasts with them in this transitory present. This much is certain: twice in the lifetimes of some of these people, once in the lifetime of nearly all of them, something was over, finished, history took a turn, made a move or a feint that made it seem as though they could start afresh, all over again, which, of course, is never really true. But that is at least how it seemed. German National Socialism was destroyed in 1945; East German Communism went bankrupt in 1989. Democracies are organised differently. They may have a beginning, but, all being well, they have no end, and this explains some of that strange feeling of temporariness and unreality that is hanging over Berlin and East Germany. In a sense, they have landed in utopia, because that was their reason for going out on to the streets: freedom, democracy, the right to have a say, everything they did not have. But now that they have it, it does not look like a utopia, except for the fact that, as with any utopia, there is no end in sight. If all goes well, this history will not be 'over' in their lifetimes, not complete, and that brings it into conflict with our human dimensions. Utopias belong in paradise, where, as we all know, it is impossible to live. Now that utopia has to happen here, it is actually proving to be something of a disappointment.

I listen in on conversations and make notes. Nothing in the following comments is invented:

The Polish professor: 'What they haven't understood here in West Germany is that capitalism has not conquered socialism but that capitalism will be socialised from the East. There's a slower movement going from East to West, and it's much more difficult to see. Incidentally, did you realise that Kohl, despite his recent defeat, is actually still in power thanks to the *Länder* of the former GDR?'

The famous feminist: 'I don't care about the taxes, just as long as they rebuild the Wall. They're different people over there, nothing to do with us. It was so different the way they grew up. This is never going to work, not in our lifetimes.'

The journalist: 'You should keep an eye open, see how many pairs of green trousers you spot in East Berlin. They may well be wearing Italian jackets, but they're wearing them with green trousers. Army issue. They can't wear the jackets, but they don't want to throw out the trousers. And if you notice that they seem to be walking a little oddly in their Adidas trainers, that's the same thing: they've been wearing army boots all their lives.'

The property owner: 'We didn't ever expect this to happen. Our family still owned a building in Erfurt. It was part of an inheritance for me and my sister. It was all managed very well. We had to pay a bill of 1,028 Deutschmarks [c. $590], but then it was ours. The estate duty had already been paid. It's estimated at almost a million. There are about fifty people living there. I should get them all to line up and submit to an inspection. No, not really. Only joking.'

The feminist: 'If at least they'd liberated themselves, the way we feminists did ... But no, even that had to come from Russia.'

The student from the East: 'My dad's brother left for the other side early on, when you still could. My dad didn't – he wanted to stay. We had a small family business, and he tried to keep it going. Once a year my uncle would come to visit us in his big Opel. And he always laughed at us because of all the things we didn't have. I hated it when he visited.'

The bookseller from the East: 'I don't need to tell you all the things that weren't allowed. But there were also loads of things that *were* allowed. Just look at the lists of titles published by Volk und Welt or Reclam. And now everything's allowed, but nothing's possible, because my shop's been bought up by a chain. Everything I know, everything I've learned, it's all become useless. You don't need to have read Updike or Goethe to sell books about sex or travel guides. And the only alternative is the door.'

The Dutch student from Leipzig: 'Before, I wasn't allowed to go to the Netherlands, and now I can't go to the Netherlands because it's too expensive. Of course, I'm happy the *Wende* [the 'turning point' in the GDR, 1989–90] happened, but it still hurts when you hear people over there saying we've got no initiative. We've got plenty of initiative, but where's that going to get you? My dad's been laid off – he'll never get another job. And it's the same everywhere. People are frightened.'

The translator from the West: 'All they know how to do is complain. It has to happen right now, it has to happen today. We didn't get things handed to us on a plate after the war either. We couldn't just head off to Majorca. They act as though we fought that war on our own. Like it was nothing to do with them. The fascists all lived in the West. And you should hear what they have to say about the Poles and Vietnamese. They're giving all of Germany a bad name.'

The Hungarian writer: 'My seven-year-old daughter was on a school trip with children from East and West Berlin. I asked her how it went. It was awful, she said. There were all these *Scheiß-Ossis* there. *Scheiß-Ossis*? Oh, they were just so stupid. Stupid? Why's that? They all looked so pathetic in their weird clothes. And what did your teachers say? Oh, our teachers never talk to their teachers.'

The photographer from Haiti: 'Racism exists wherever you go, but I had a good life here in Berlin for thirty-three years. That's over now, my friend. I don't dare go to the East any more, not in the daytime and definitely not at night. People have been stabbed and thrown off the train. Dead, I mean. There were a lot of Mozambicans and Angolans living there, solidarity between the nations – you know, all that stuff. They were always invited to march past the tribune with everyone else on May Day. But they treated them like slaves even before, and now they've got to leave. There's no work. They were all part of the old regime, of course. Not their fault, but that's how people see it now. *Ausländer raus*, good riddance.' ✒

High Infidelity

Many tourists begin their exploration of Berlin at Checkpoint Charlie, a replica of the border post that was already long gone by the time the Wall came down. In some ways this sums up perfectly the city's architectonic history from the post-war period to the present day. From a copy of the Palazzo Borghese to a faithful reconstruction of the Hohenzollern Castle, Berlin celebrates a past that it does not own.

THIBAUT DE RUYTER
Translated by Tina Kover

Left: 'Say cheese!' In front of Checkpoint Charlie, now known affectionately by the nickname 'Snackpoint Charlie' (see the famous fast-food outlet to the right).

ONE BALCONY, TWO BALCONIES

If you visit Berlin's famous Museum Island to admire Nefertiti or the paintings of Caspar David Friedrich, you will also find a particularly interesting spot which, all by itself, encapsulates the whole of Berlin – and the whole of this article. Coming from Unter den Linden and turning your back to the Brandenburg Gate, stop after a few metres on the Schlossbrücke, preferably on the left-hand side, and look to your right. The first thing you'll see, of course, is the newly completed Berliner Schloss, the Berlin Palace. The building, its scaffolding taken down, has found its place in the urban landscape. It exists (even if a certain virus postponed its official opening and – at the time I write these lines – I still haven't managed to get inside). Pause here, on the bridge, and look carefully. This part of the city has changed radically in the past twenty-five years. Here in 1976 East Germany unveiled its Palast der Republik (a multi-purpose building that included the committee room of the East German Parliament, an auditorium, a post office, exhibition spaces, restaurants and cafés, a theatre and even a bowling alley). Nothing remains of that building today or of numerous other edifices aside from the old Staatsratsgebäude (State Council Building), which is now an international technology and management school. All around the Palace, with its smells of fresh paint, in an area that presents itself as the historic heart of the German capital, false history reigns. But if you look carefully at the side of the Palace facing Unter den Linden and then at the front of the management school, something should catch your eye: an entire stretch of their respective façades is identical. This is because, in 1950, when East Germany decided to demolish the Palace, a symbol of rightist, warmongering Prussia, it preserved a fragment of the building: the portal and balcony where, on 9 November 1918, Karl Liebknecht proclaimed the Free Socialist Republic of Germany. This architectural element was then moved by the GDR and incorporated into a new, modern edifice that today houses the European School of Management and Technology. It's a good idea when you're erasing history to demonstrate your discerning tastes and save whatever is symbolically deserving. But the most amusing part of this story is that during the reconstruction of the Palace façade the decision was made not to dismantle this authentic segment and incorporate it back into the 'historic' Palace but rather to create a replica less than two hundred metres from the original. Result: Berlin now has two balconies for the price of one! (And, if you continue your examination, you can even treat yourself to a game of spot the difference …)

PRIDE

I don't think another situation quite like this exists anywhere else in the world. There is a Statue of Liberty in Paris, a great pyramid in Las Vegas and an Eiffel Tower in Almaty, Kazakhstan, but if we take this urban comedy as a starting point it quickly becomes clear that we are really looking at a

THIBAUT DE RUYTER is a French-German architect, curator and art critic, who has lived and worked in Berlin since 2001. He has written for magazines such as *L'Architecture d'aujourd'hui*, *Artpress*, *Il giornale dell'architettura*, *Fucking Good Art*, *architectuul* and *Frieze d/e*. In addition to curating numerous international exhibitions – including *A Song for Europe* at the Victoria and Albert Museum, London, 2017 – he has edited a number of books on architecture, including *Stadt / bild* (Verbrecher Verlag, 2015).

'Everyone is smiling, imagining themselves to be participating in a historical moment. But what history is this exactly?'

retroactive manifesto for the city of Berlin (to co-opt the subtitle of Rem Koolhaas's 1978 book *Delirious New York*). One just needs to stand at the right spot on a particular bridge to see two identical balconies, at which point fantasies of copies, originals, history, stories and stupidity will arise.

YOU ARE LEAVING THE AMERICAN SECTOR (ALMOST)

Ludwig Feuerbach, in his preface to the second edition of *The Essence of Christianity* (1841), wrote: 'Certainly … the present age … prefers the sign to the thing signified, the copy to the original, the fancy to reality, the appearance to the essence … in these days *illusion* only is *sacred*, truth *profane*. Nay, sacredness is held to be enhanced in proportion as truth decreases and illusion increases, so that the highest degree of illusion comes to be the highest degree of sacredness.' Guy Debord cites this quote in his famous 1967 book *The Society of the Spectacle*, and while his thesis focused principally on Paris and Florence, if one looks at the way Berlin manipulated both copies and originals during the second half of the 20th century, it's impossible not to think of that city, too.

So let's head to the spot where hundreds of thousands of visitors begin their stay in Berlin: Checkpoint Charlie. It's impossible to miss the small border post in the middle of the road; impossible to avoid ending up in a photo snapped by some Japanese tourist; impossible to resist buying a souvenir postcard there with a real fragment of the Berlin Wall embedded in it! It sits in the middle of Friedrichstrasse where it intersects with Zimmerstrasse: a

traffic island, a modest white wooden hut, sandbags filled with concrete, a double-sided photograph on the top of a pole showing a US officer and a Soviet soldier and more than a few street hawkers peddling fur hats adorned with a hammer and sickle, badges with Lenin's face on them and GDR Army belt-buckles. It occurs to me to wonder whether, thirty-plus years after the Wall came down, these objects are still being mass-produced in some secret, well-guarded Brandenburg factory for tourists hungry for 'authentic' souvenirs. Two or three actors in the uniform of the Grepo (the GDR's border police) will, for a few euros, pose for photographs alongside British travellers in shorts or stamp their passports with an entry visa for a country that no longer exists. Everyone is smiling, imagining themselves to be participating in a historical moment. But what history is this exactly? Does it possess even the faintest whiff of truth?

THE WHITE CABIN DEEP IN THE WOODS

Almost no trace of the Wall remains in the city, and only a discerning eye can still pick out – by the design of a street lamp or the way in which a pavement is constructed – differences between West Berlin and East Berlin (you can also tell by the presence of trams [former East] or the ethnicity of the vendors in the *Späti*, Berlin convenience stores that stay open into the wee hours). The first Checkpoint Charlie was built by the Americans to monitor the comings and goings between the Soviet sector and the zone occupied by Allied forces; it is in the middle of Friedrichstrasse, which runs through two different quarters

Above: Berlin Cathedral (at the right of the picture) and the two faces of the Berlin Palace: the historic façade and the modern Humboldt Forum.

(Mitte to the north [East] and Kreuzberg to the south [West]), and was thus naturally divided between the Allied and Soviet zones. It quickly became necessary to provide a structure several square metres in area to shelter the military personnel in charge of passport control, and from there the sentry-box evolved over the years, being renovated and improved, modified and rebuilt, becoming larger and, as the Cold War intensified, more high security. Shortly after the fall of the Berlin Wall the building was transported to the Allied

Museum on Clayallee in the borough of Zehlendorf, well outside the city centre. In 2000, to please the crowds of tourists who travelled to the original spot and found nothing, it was decided to 'rebuild' Checkpoint Charlie as it had been in the early 1960s – without exactly broadcasting the fact that the structure that stands on the site is only a copy of an original that disappeared long before the fall of the Wall. Certainly the more well-informed tourist guides point this out, but who would want to travel several thousand kilometres just to see a replica? The visitor desperate for authenticity, though, will make their way to the Allied Museum, located in a former movie theatre built for occupying US troops that is set in a lovely forest clearing. There, you can also find a French military train carriage, a British Handley Page Hastings aeroplane (reg. TG503) dating from the 1948 Berlin Airlift, a real prefabricated concrete East German watchtower and the final version of Checkpoint Charlie (part of the very first checkpoint is also on display). Important note: entry to the Allied Museum is free, while an adult ticket to the Mauermuseum (the Wall Museum) at the reconstructed Checkpoint Charlie costs €14.50 ($17.50)! Unfortunately, the Allied Museum is in the middle of nowhere and rarely figures in tourist walking itineraries. Worst of all, you can't even buy a piece of the Wall in the gift shop.

DISNEYLAND ON THE SPREE (PART ONE)

The story of the replica Checkpoint Charlie neatly sums up the history of a large part of Berlin (and many other German cities) since the Second World War: historical traces are most often reconstructions, more or less accurate copies and roughly approximate restorations. Yet it seems never to occur to anyone to mention this fact or put up a notice stating it, much less

to question the existence of these historical fibs, because the copies are good for the collective psyche, soothing the sore places and scars left by History. And so tourists are left to stroll through a vast Disneyland they believe to be authentic, while politicians, whether out of sheer demagoguery or desperation for votes, allow themselves to get bogged down in absurd projects like the reconstruction of the Berlin Palace.

THE TRUEST COPY IN BERLIN

A stone's throw from Checkpoint Charlie, around three hundred metres, stands an entire city block built by Aldo Rossi in the mid-1990s, the Quartier Schützenstrasse. At number 8 on this street you will find the loveliest copy in all of Berlin. Even though its details are not, on closer examination, of the highest quality, clashing outrageously with the decor, this is a re-created section of the courtyard-facing façade of the Palazzo Farnese in Rome, designed and built by Antonio Sangallo in 1515 and modified by Michelangelo in 1546. As Rossi was designing and building over a full city block, he decided to break his façades up into a number of individual buildings (and addresses). Something between a collage, a pastiche and a tribute, this allowed him to create a subtler link between his architecture and the city, one less massive and overwhelming. (By way of contrast, to see an example of how architects can come up with successful solutions for a single block-sized building, one should just carry on along the street to reach the new Springer building by Rem Koolhaas and OMA.) This may not be the most elegant or well constructed of Aldo Rossi's creations, but with this falsely true copy he pushes postmodernism to its limits, confining himself to building what already exists elsewhere in history. This assemblage of façades, which lacks the graphic simplicity of the

THE PASSENGER   Thibaut de Ruyter

Pariser Platz, which was completely rebuilt in the 2000s. During the Cold War the only structure near the Brandenburg Gate was the Berlin Wall.

(many) buildings he designed for the IBA87 (International Building Exhibition Berlin 1987), is symptomatic of what Berlin was ready to become after the fall of the Wall: a more or less haphazard, more or less interpretative, more or less careful copy of its past self, with the ultimate goal of erasing every trace both of the bombardments of the Second World War and of the GDR. But it lost any semblance of humour or irony along the way, the idea of copying taken too literally, seriousness and ostentation increasing as truth decreased.

LEAVING CHECKPOINT CHARLIE

But what do the tourists do after leaving Checkpoint Charlie? In which direction do they point themselves? Probably not east or west, for Zimmerstrasse is a rather depressing and unwelcoming prospect. Aldo Rossi's block does not feature in the guidebooks, and visitors are unlikely to find it on their own. Friedrichstrasse heading south is no better. This leaves them to set off north, crossing the terrifying Leipziger Strasse to find, on their right, the elegant black-glass Galeries Lafayette building designed by Jean Nouvel, with its lavishly dressed holograms. Proceeding onwards they will reach Unter den Linden only to find that here, too, very little of note awaits them. No, Berlin is definitely not a city for strolling around. You hop on a bike, and you go where you need to go. But, that being said, the courageous walker who turns left on to Unter den Linden towards the Brandenburg Gate will find more attractive copies – less symptomatic than the brand-new Palace but just as firmly nestled into the urban landscape. The Hotel Adlon, for example, inaugurated in 1997, is only a rough approximation, a building 'in the style of' the one that stood on the site before the war. The same is true of the two buildings that flank the Brandenburg

Gate, Haus Liebermann and Haus Sommer, designed by architect Josef Paul Kleihues and constructed in 1999. The Pariser Platz is a perfect example of modern Berlin's architectural expectations: heavy, falsely historic, dull and uncontroversial. But this square also lends itself to a game that is fun for all ages: spotting errors and architectural details that betray the true dates of (re-)construction, or examining archival images to see how the buildings shown there became modern buildings ashamed of their own modernity. Belly laughs guaranteed. Anyone who, desiring to escape this misery, turns right off Friedrichstrasse will quickly reach number 1 Unter den Linden, which faces the Bertelsmann building, the Kommandantenhaus, also a dubious copy, completed in 2003. This construction undoubtedly provided the inspiration for the reconstruction of the Berlin Palace, proving that it was both viable and plausible; here it was no longer a matter of interpreting, imagining or designing 'in the style of' but one of rebuilding an actual replica using archival documents (most often watercolour street views). But where the Hotel Adlon admits, to the careful observer, that it is only a copy, the Bertelsmann building claims the greatest authenticity; the most amusing part of any tour of the place is discovering the heavy modern wall of glass that opens out on to the rear courtyard. Three 'historic' sides and a 'modern' one – a solution also recommended in the case of the Palace. Berlin wants to create a historical and historicising image for itself but not without the must-have amenities of maximum natural daylight, air conditioning and ultra-fast broadband. What began with Checkpoint Charlie and the reconstruction of the military guardhouse to please the tourists has gradually crept outwards to encompass the whole city. And now, insidiously, on every street corner, the worm has taken up residence in the fruit.

DISNEYLAND ON THE SPREE (PART TWO)

Another spot of particular attraction to tourists is the Nikolaiviertel, which is just behind the Berlin Palace on the other side of the Spree next to the Rotes Rathaus (town hall). It's worth remembering that it was here, between 1220 and 1230, that Berlin was founded, making it one of the oldest and most historic parts of the city. Unfortunately, however, almost none of the buildings that made up these few streets survived the bombardments of the Second World War – and it was not until 1987 and the city's 750th anniversary that East Berlin took any interest in the area at all. With tourist guides insisting on the importance of encouraging visits to the quarter, the GDR decided to rebuild it, keeping to the original street plan and buildings. But what is really fantastic here are the prefabricated concrete panels, the 'two-bit' reconstruction. East Germany had industrialised its architecture in the 1960s, manufacturing concrete building slabs in factories with windows fixed and wallpaper already hung. These panels were then transported in trucks to the building sites and rapidly assembled. Speed, thrift, efficiency and standardisation were the key words of the process, known as *Plattenbauten*; of course, it was also synonymous with monotony and a lack of aesthetic creativity. In the 1980s the GDR made the decision to decorate these slabs, adding bow windows and even coming up with models capable of supporting pitched roofs – although a wide silicon joint still betrayed their method of construction. This type of building was subsequently used for a large number of Nikolaiviertel's structures, despite its obvious shoddiness and modernity. And, as it turned out, the

Above: The two towers of Frankfurter Tor: a nod to Prussian history in the midst of the Stalinist architecture of Karl-Marx-Allee, with a clear reference to the neoclassical domes of the Gendarmenmarkt's German and French cathedrals.

historic monuments commission was not fooled (or, perhaps, decided to display a bit of irony): the quarter is now classed not as a 13th-century site but as an example of a particular era of construction in the German Democratic Republic. In the end some buildings were reconstructed a few dozen metres from their original locations, as in the case of the Ephraim Palace, while others made more effort to hide their true nature but remain feeble imitations that wouldn't even be credible as film sets. All you have to do is get close and

THE PASSENGER Thibaut de Ruyter

touch them to feel their 'lightness', and, if you give them a tap, they make the same hollow sound as Aldo Rossi's façade near Checkpoint Charlie. This is architecture that quite literally rings false, with the entertaining, slightly ridiculous beauty of the replica that admits to being one, that realises it will never be anything but a simulacrum and doesn't attempt to lie to itself – and that ends up, a few decades later, as a listed historic monument.

A RUSSIAN COPY

Another lovely copy from the period of Soviet occupation in Berlin can be found a bit further east, in the middle of Karl-Marx-Allee: the two towers of the Frankfurter Tor, built in the 1950s in imitation of the Gendarmenmarkt towers constructed by Carl von Gontard between 1780 and 1785. But Berlin, a city whose history is mostly recent and which did not truly flourish until the late 19th century, is unable to base its urban image on a long and glorious past; it must, then, seek its history elsewhere, appropriating anything and everything for its own use as a matter of course. So when in 1951 East Berlin began to plan the reconstruction of the Frankfurter Allee to turn it into Stalinallee, a great symbolic boulevard beginning at Alexanderplatz and running east towards Poland and, symbolically, the Soviet Union, the authorities commissioned Hermann Henselmann to create something that would please the occupiers. He obliged with the beautiful Haus an der Weberwiese, which would serve as an aesthetic basis for all of the architects responsible for the various blocks of the Stalinallee. (East Berlin had organised a study trip to Moscow in December 1949 to help provide the architects with sources of inspiration.) Henselmann's creation – marked by Schinkelesque classicism, a melange of didactic ornamental details

A DREAM, AN OBSESSION

Long before the dispute broke out between those who wanted to rebuild the Berlin Palace and those who wanted to save the GDR parliament building, before the Wall came down – in fact, not long after it was built – a man by the name of Wilhelm von Boddien began to collect every possible document concerning the Palace, becoming the greatest expert on the building and, later, the principal advocate for its resurrection. Not that his battle was a popular one; far from it: in the beginning he was taken for a madman. Perhaps he was obsessed or, on the other hand, perhaps he was a visionary who imagined the re-emergence of the Palace's façades when such a thing still seemed inconceivable. When the rumour spread in the early 1990s that an association was fighting for the Palace to be rebuilt, it immediately triggered a wave of protest, indignation and fear about the return of Prussia. But after the initial suspicion wore off, Von Boddien and his friends acted shrewdly to form a lobby. They courted politicians and, above all, the people of Berlin by means of a stunt: a gigantic life-sized painting showing the Palace's façade that temporarily gave passers-by on Unter den Linden the illusion that the royal residence had reappeared at the end of the tree-lined avenue. In the end, following on from the success of Potsdamer Platz, the strategy of transforming the project and then the construction works into a spectacle was once again able to sway public opinion. In 2011 a futuristic temporary building complete with trendy rooftop bar was even constructed to present the future plans for the area. Known as the Humboldt Box, it was taken down in 2018.

and faience tiles with symbolic decoration (such as the sheaves of wheat that were such an important element of Stalin's five-year plans) – is a striking expression of socialist realism applied to architecture. While Berlin may pride itself on possessing one of the longest historical monuments in the world (the whole of what is now Karl-Marx-Allee, formerly Stalinallee, is listed as a single monument), and even though this monument is in a style shared with almost no other city apart from Moscow and Warsaw, it is merely an appropriation, a series of samples, borrowings and copies taken from the East. And, in the end, there is very little real difference between appropriation and copying.

AN ORIGINAL COPY, DISPLACED AND DERIVED

In 1998, in keeping with the common tendency of relying heavily on references in his search for symbolic value, Hans Kollhoff designed one of the towers in the highly publicised Potsdamer Platz (see 'The Greatest Show in Town' on page 13). But Kollhoff's copy draws on semantic and stylistic relocation and, in this, it is as whimsical and misplaced as the work of Aldo Rossi. Its tower is clad in red brick, a material rarely visible in the city of Berlin as it is always encased in plaster. Its structure is far more evocative of Louis Sullivan's USA than it is of Erich Mendelsohn's Berlin. One can't truly say that Kollhoff copies anyone else, but, like the good postmodernist that he is, he seeks references far from Berlin to validate the existence of his tower in a city that possesses almost none of them. A bit like Schinkel (who spent his time gazing towards Italy for inspiration) and the architects of Karl-Marx-Allee on their study trip to Moscow and Rossi (moving a fragment of Rome to Berlin), Kollhoff is proving that he is cultured. But, once

again, he is reinforcing the point that, if the new German capital wishes to find a history for itself, it must seek it elsewhere and not on its own soil.

AUTHENTICITY

Berlin's copies are never wholly authentic; they are an interpretation, a new invention, a game of form and style based on a few archival documents used to justify politicians' speeches, investors' interests, architects' inspiration and public appetite. The ultimate proof of all of this lies, of course, in the reconstruction of the Berlin Palace. I will not test the reader's patience by recounting the endless debates that took place between those for and against the endeavour; suffice it to say that at the turn of the millennium not a day passed without a new article appearing in the press, one report following another so quickly that they cancelled each other out (fortunately, following the resounding and repeated failures of Berlin Brandenburg Airport the papers were spoiled for choice both for fake news and actual disasters). It's worth remembering, though, that the decision was made to recreate *ex nihilo* three of the Palace's four historic façades and to let the Italian architect Franco Stella design the building's interior in the modern-historic-corporate style so popular throughout Berlin and much of Germany today. What we have been left with is the most slapdash and problematic kind of façadism, which occurs when there isn't even a façade left to restore, preserve or protect. Instead, everything must be invented on the basis of a few black-and-white images and a pile of random documents. This building marks the end of the history of architecture. It is no longer a question of modernity or postmodernity, no longer a question of 'critical reconstruction' or gentle urban integration, no longer a question of playing

The controversial Palace, redesigned by the Italian architect Franco Stella, is now home to the Humboldt Forum, a new multi-functional cultural hub that further enriches Museum Island's already impressive range of attractions with the addition of the Ethnological Museum and the Museum of Asian Art, which have previously suffered from being located in the outlying district of Dahlem. According to Neil MacGregor, former director of the British Museum and director of the founding directorate for the Berlin project, 'the museum's collections will serve as a basis to understand global interconnections and perceive the world as a whole, in the Humboldtian spirit'. The Palace is also used by Humboldt University as an experimental research facility as well as hosting a permanent exhibition about the city. In classic Berlin style, the opening of the complex has already been put back three times (once because of Covid-19), and, in the meantime, the Humboldt Forum has also been dragged into the controversies sparked by French president Emmanuel Macron's declarations during a visit to Senegal in 2017, when he expressed his desire to return art that was plundered from Africa during the colonial period. Bénédicte Savoy, one of the former directors of the Humboldt Forum, resigned from her post in protest at the museum's attitude to works of art appropriated during colonial times, stating that before opening stringent checks on their provenance should be carried out. 'I want to know how much blood is dripping from each artwork,' she declared.

around with citations. For architects the world over, the opening of the Palace will sound the death knell: their research, their dogma and their follies will be swept aside, condemned to non-existence; all they will have to do is build a city on the basis of a few historical documents unearthed in archives by researchers. The real problem isn't so much that the Palace is being built in Berlin (after all, the city will have what it chooses to have and what it deserves, and it is welcome to it), its tragedy lies in the ability to say, 'Look, it's entirely possible, and you can do the same in your city!' In this way the Berlin syndrome will infect the whole world. The 1970s – which saw the construction of Ralf Schüler and Ursulina Schüler-Witte's International Congress Centre (ICC 1979), Ludwig Leo's Institute of Naval Engineering (1976) on the edge of the Tiergarten and Věra and Vladimír Machonin's Czech embassy (1978) in East Berlin not far from Checkpoint Charlie at 44 Wilhelmstrasse; so many different architectural approaches, whether or not to everyone's taste, that shared the same spark of creativity, futurism and experimentation – are a thing of the past. Once the Palace is complete, lovers of history will insist on their own right to build, anywhere and everywhere, 'the way they did in the good old days' with 'the beautiful methods of yesteryear', and in so doing they will give *carte blanche* to investors and politicians who, even now, sometimes attempt to defy voters' wishes and construct an urban utopia or an architectural form that rubs public opinion up the wrong way. Why not build replicas of the Tour de Nesle or the Bastille or Les Halles of Baltard – not to mention the roof of Notre-Dame? No need to have new ideas or take risks any more: the solution to all our problems is to copy the past freely. Tremble at the thought, my brethren.

Below: The Palace in a photograph dating from 1891.

RÜCKBAU

Koolhaas's book *Delirious New York* concludes with an appendix featuring a number of short architectural fairy tales, written by Rem Koolhaas and illustrated by Madelon Vriesendorp. Here the architect's offerings include a swimming pool in the form of a floating barge; capable of crossing the Atlantic from Moscow to New York, the pool is powered by those swimming in it – so long as they swim in the opposite direction to that of travel, according to the principle in physics that for every action there is an equal and opposite reaction. The word *Rückbau* was used regularly during the demolition of the Palast der Republik. Combining the idea of construction, *Bau*, with the German prefix *rück*, meaning 'backwards', it evokes the process of dismantling, deconstruction, rather than a dramatic dynamiting, even though the end result is the same: the complete annihilation of the building. It represents the ultimate victory of the politically correct ambience surrounding the slow but inexorable removal of every trace of the GDR; the Palast wasn't demolished but taken apart, piece by piece – a dismantling that avoids the production of spectacular and symbolic images such as the ones shown on television when the towers and border fences on the outskirts of the city were blown up. The Palast vanished slowly, discreetly, insidiously.

But, like Rem Koolhaas, we could imagine another plan for the forty-four hectares of land across from Museum Island. During the years between the demolition of the original Palace in 1950 and the opening of the Palast der Republik in 1976, the site remained vacant. The *Rückbau* of the Palast lasted from 1998 to 2008 and, until construction work on the Palace began, the spot was occupied by a spacious green esplanade featuring a few archaeological remnants of foundations and a truly awful temporary pavilion intended to serve as a placeholder for the reconstructed Palace. In late 2020 the scaffolding came down and work continued on the interior ahead of a step-by-step opening in 2021. All we would need to do is turn back our watches and make the hands of the clock run anti-clockwise to deconstruct the Palace and then reconstruct the Palast der Republik in exactly the same amount of time (ten years, 1998–2008) it took to take it down. According to this, the new building would remain on this site for the next twenty-two years and then be dismantled in the same time it took for it to be built in the mid-1970s (thirty-two months). The land would remain vacant again for twenty-three years, after which, during the course of a single night, the time it took for its demolition, the Palace would once again appear just as it was in 1950, complete with the scars inflicted by Allied bombs. We would then have to wait until 2085 to restore it to how it was before the first bombardments of Berlin. Next, still in compliance with the most exact historical chronology possible, the rooms and wings of the Palace and its surroundings would shift and change, appearing and disappearing according to the various developments and transformations to which the original site was subject during its lifespan (only in reverse order), until, eight centuries from now, we would be back to a time when Berlin was merely a few houses on an island in the Spree and absolutely nothing would remain. History, wholly reversed and replayed, would end in a murky and marshy landscape. This pharaonic exercise, hardly more absurd than swimming against the current in a floating swimming pool or, for that matter, deciding to reconstruct a building that hasn't existed in more than sixty years, would create

Checkpoint Charlie, seen from
the US sector of Friedrichstrasse.

'In Berlin, a city where copying has become the rule, an original is now the exception. But these originals have also fallen victim to another Berlin outbreak: the relocation of buildings within the city.'

work for dozens of architects, hundreds of historians, a whole host of engineers and thousands of construction workers on a perpetual building site. It would become Berlin's ultimate tourist attraction, a copy created in real time, an unparalleled treat for visitors in search of history in a city that possesses almost none.

GOING CRAZY

Berlin is indeed going a little crazy, but its delirium lacks the beauty of New York's. In the German capital it is synonymous with stupidity, with a lack of vision, with fear of the void and demagoguery towards public opinion. What if Checkpoint Charlie were to be rebuilt again, this time with the trappings of the East Berlin border post with its watchtowers and its guards with their dogs and rifles? Another tourist attraction would finally be complete.

SMALL PACTS WITH THE DEAD

And now it's time for me to reveal one final trick. When East Germany decided to preserve the section of façade and Karl Liebknecht's famous balcony, it made a fatal error. Before demolishing the rest of the building the portal had been packed with straw to protect it from the explosions, but this proved to be insufficient insulation from the blast and, once the straw was removed, all that remained was a pile of unusable bricks and stones. The fragment of façade that is now part of the management school is a different one, one that did survive the demolition – but not that from which Karl Liebknecht spoke to

the masses. Everyone is curiously reluctant to tell this story, of course, and History wants it to be the authentic balcony. In Berlin, a city where copying (or loosely interpreting a historical original) has become the rule, an original is now the exception. But these originals have also fallen victim to another Berlin outbreak: the relocation of buildings within the city. The Victory Column, for example, which was moved to the middle of the Grosser Stern in 1938, was previously located next to the Reichstag. Aldo Rossi, as we have seen, relocated a fragment of the Palazzo Farnese, while the original Checkpoint Charlie was transported to the Allied Museum. While it is normally a matter of course to divide goods into movable and immovable categories, into what moves and what does not, Berlin's architecture, it seems, shifts around time and place more easily than its residents.

A PALACE, A CASTLE, A CATHEDRAL …

The city's manipulation of its own history (and its own architecture) has no equivalent anywhere else in the world – certainly not on the same scale or with so many examples. But now it is Notre-Dame, Paris, that faces questions over the possible reconstruction of its roof. (The methods and reference date for restoration will have to be selected; do we restore the appearance of the cathedral from before or after the mid-19th-century modifications made by Viollet-le-Duc?) There will undoubtedly be dozens of proposals and counter-proposals seeking to oppose the desire for history and

nostalgia for a destroyed past. Berlin can serve as an example, sharing its knowledge by announcing loudly and clearly, 'Look, we've managed to produce identical reconstructions of three façades of our Palace; you can do the same with your roof!' But no one will dare ask the question as to what purpose a palace or a cathedral truly serves, here at the beginning of the 21st century.

RED LINGERIE AND A PEAKED CAP

In 2012 a brand of lingerie, the name of which I can't remember, launched a soft attack on Checkpoint Charlie. A lovely young woman, (un)dressed in a set of matching red underwear and proudly sporting an East German military cap, posed for a photographer in front of the little sentry-box with its fresh coat of white paint. The event made passers-by smile; nothing malicious or blasphemous about it. The photographs of the phoney historical monument and the phoney soldier; the phoney cleavage and the phoney scandal quickly made the rounds on the internet and in the press, only to be forgotten the next day. If Berlin were, finally, to establish a retroactive manifesto for itself like the one Rem Koolhaas created for New York, it would be here; the era of Feuerbach and Debord has gone. It is no longer a question of preferring the copy to the original or even of trying to tell them apart; it is enough simply to like the copy without knowing a destroyed or displaced original even existed; to generate information that will be obsolete even before it is absorbed. In this topsy-turvy world, truth is merely a stage of falsehood. That is Berlin's manifesto. 🐦

In the Belly of the Whale

Before Covid-19 closed all the city's nightspots, journalist Juliane Löffler spent an evening at the most transgressive venue on the Berlin scene, the KitKat sex club. Here's how her evening panned out.

JULIANE LÖFFLER
Translated by Claudio Cambon
Illustrations by Felix Scheinberger

127

It smells of hot sex. Someone is sitting on a bench next to me unlacing her boots, and in the background a woman leads a man by the chain-link collar around his neck. Somewhere, water is splashing.

Did we know where we were, the doorman asked, a giant of a man in a bomber jacket, because from the outside the KitKat looks pretty drab and innocuous with its grey, concrete walls. But that innocuousness dissipates the moment you step inside, because you smell nightclub and sex right away. It's cramped and warm, and the heated bodies bump up against the newcomers who have entered on this ordinary Saturday evening. It's as if we have all ended up together in the belly of the whale.

A woman stands next to me wearing a black-lace bodysuit that readily reveals her breasts and labia. At the cloakroom, a small group of men talk to the attendant in English. She is wearing a leather harness around her hips and no underwear. A glass filled with lollipops sits on the counter in front of her. 'Yes, the T-shirts definitely have to come off,' she says. 'Give us a schnapps if we go naked,' they begin to haggle. They argue about their boxer shorts. Fetish, leather or nude – that's the dress code. Goth and glamour are OK, too, but not jeans.

We have come to the KitKat, a name that tourists whisper reverently when talking about Berlin's club scene. At the front door the boss, Kirsten Krüger, barely fifty, selects the guests. Many years ago, she and her friend Simon Thaur from Austria founded the club 'for civilised people'. They named it after the wicked establishment in the musical *Cabaret*. And for twenty-seven years the place has stood for sex, excess, hedonism, for Berlin itself, because freedom for all reigns here, or maybe it's just because a few ground rules hold the place together. One of so many loose ends in this city, this is somewhere that doesn't belong to anything other than itself.

We have stripped down to our plain black panties. My friend has put strips of gaffer tape over her nipples. We've checked everything in except for a few one-euro tokens that we stuff into our socks as we round the corner. We scout the place like wide-eyed little kids, working our way past the many sweaty bodies through a labyrinth of rooms and side rooms. The place is full. Psychedelic paintings shimmer on the walls. Pole-dancing podiums and booths surround the dance floors. A woman wearing neon-bright lacy underwear dances up against a pole, pressing her backside against the metal and looking around the room invitingly. A woman walks up, then a man, their lips and bodies quivering with desire. A small balcony above them wraps around the dance floor, where we spy bodies slapping against each other rhythmically – a semi-public orgy hovering over us. We don't feel like joining them. Watching is OK, staring feels stupid, but taking part is always allowed. I see a leg and a hip; through the smoke on the stage a man in full body paint walks up the stairs with determination. In one of the back rooms we come across a bondage show where a woman writhes, red ropes pinching her body tightly. We sit

JULIANE LÖFFLER is a journalist who specialises in LGBT rights and feminism for BuzzFeed news. Previously she worked on the editorial board of the weekly *Der Freitag*. Her work has been published in the *Guardian* and by the publishers Suhrkamp and Transcript. She is a fellow of the Reporters in the Field programme of the Robert Bosch foundation and a fellow of the International Alumni Center (IAC Berlin).

ENTRANCE AROUND the CORNER

BRAVE NEW WORLD

The Covid-19 pandemic has hit the nightclub scene especially hard, and clubs have
done whatever they can to survive, through online initiatives such as United We Stream
or by reinventing themselves. During the summer of 2020, those that had outdoor
spaces turned into *Biergärten* where punters could listen to electronic music while
seated: dancing was forbidden. Two long-standing institutions of Berlin's nightlife
took very different paths: Berghain made a virtue out of necessity by transforming
itself into an art exhibition space in collaboration with the Boros Foundation, while
the KitKat, the subject of this article, became a centre for rapid Covid tests.

In the Belly of the Whale

BERLIN
30/4/16

down. A man offers me a lap dance, but I refuse, thanking him anyway. We want to understand the place before we use it. We head for the swimming-pool room, which is humid and smells faintly of chlorine. The light-blue water casts luminous reflections on the walls. Several guests sit along the edge, dangling their legs in the water. It's as if everyone is waiting for something to happen. This room is legendary. Everyone who talks about the KitKat talks about the swimming pool and the big swing that hangs over it, because *anything* can happen here. Or nothing at all. Somehow, the water represents all the bodily fluids mixing here tonight. It's both repulsive and erotic.

We dance, we laugh, we gape in astonishment, and after just one hour our initial shyness gives way to a sense of normality, as if this were a sauna where no one is surprised by the nudity and the only remarkable thing is seeing people putting their clothes back on afterwards in the changing room.

For decades subculture niches like the KitKat survived and thrived in Berlin, because the city, a West German island smack in the middle of East Germany, ringed by walls, was able to flout many of the rules that applied elsewhere. This was a place for people who wanted to do things differently or who simply didn't fit in anywhere else. People came to Berlin because there was no mandatory community service and no closing time – instead, plenty of breathing space. As a result, even

'In twenty-five years the KitKat has not had a single complaint of sexual misconduct. Perhaps it doesn't ever happen, which would be quite unusual for a nightclub.'

today, the club scene is queer and very diverse; there are places for spanking, swingers, dark rooms with names like Böse Buben (Bad boys), Silverfuture and Ficken 3000 (Fuck 3000). The freedom they provide is queer because they don't follow the heteronormative rules by which our society largely lives. This is where people mingle to play out their desires with one another.

At some point my friend vanished as I made my way through the rooms, gin and tonic in hand, contemplating flabby bellies bulging out from thongs on one side and taut six-packs on the other. People lie on the red upholstered chairs, masturbating, French kissing, fondling each other. The bodies are so diverse, as they are in real life and as they aren't in pornography. I see young students, seasoned swingers, ample women, bearded men, gay, straight and, in between, anyone who refuses to categorise their sexuality in any way. The queer Sunday after-hours party here used to be called the Freak Show, and now it is simply known as the Peep Show. Leaning against the bar is Herbert, who has been coming here for fifteen years. With his light-grey hair, beer belly and the thick leather bands that adorn his wrists, he chats away happily with the female bartender as if he were in some regular neighbourhood bar and not standing among a bunch of naked people.

'Can I watch?' I turn around to see a young man, perhaps just a few years older than me, as I lean in the doorway, waiting for a toilet to free up. He's pretty, with his silver earrings and tousled blond hair. I

don't understand. 'What do you mean?' I ask him. He asks me whether I am waiting to use the toilet, and if I have to go for a number one or two. 'I have to pee,' I tell him. He again asks me, 'Can I watch?' I feel the alcohol. My body feels lighter than usual and, amazingly, I find the question reasonable and not intrusive. Consent culture. In twenty-five years the KitKat has not had a single complaint of sexual misconduct. Perhaps it doesn't ever happen, which would be quite unusual for a nightclub.

So I take the guy with the tousled hair with me into the small toilet cubicle. He squeezes into the corner and begins to fumble with his fly. As my urine splashes loudly in the toilet bowl, he looks at the underpants pinched in between my knees and begins to masturbate and moan. Suddenly it's too much for me. Perhaps it's because I just don't understand fetish culture or perhaps I have just become aware of the intimacy within this tiny space, just two metres square. 'You have to leave,' I tell him, opening the door latch before he manages to pack his dick away properly. I stumble out of the toilet and find my friend, her head buried in another woman's neck. I tap her on the shoulder. 'This is Lena,' she says, pointing to the woman. We kiss each other on the cheek, and I quickly tell her what just happened. We laugh. I wander off again into the crowd on the dance floor and watch a group of young gay men wearing briefs with a small opening at the rear, their six-packs smeared with gold glitter. 'Welcome to the unicorns,' one of them says. I let my hand brush against the glitter and join their

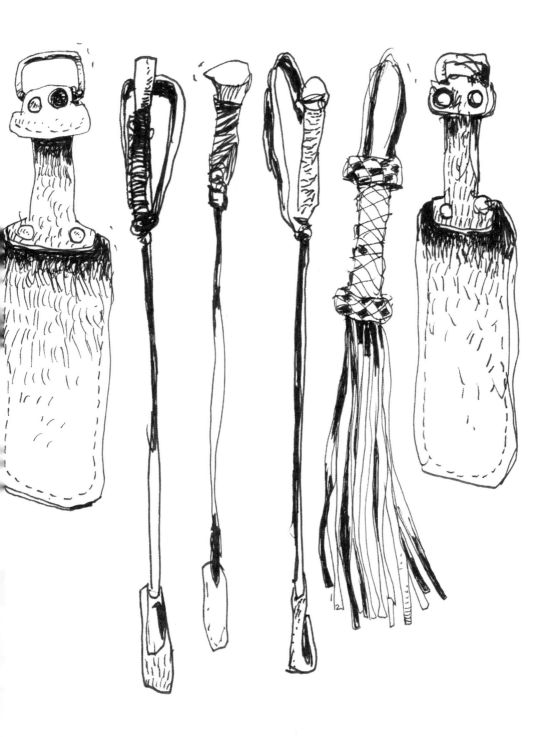

In the Belly of the Whale

dance circle. We exchange compliments and shake our bodies to the beat.

A permeable, parallel culture has sprung forth at the KitKat, essentially because anyone is welcome here, be they curious party people looking for adventure or experienced sex clubbers who know where all the real hard-core places are in Berlin. Some come for the exoticism and others to feel at home. Somehow the KitKat manages to preserve its identity, despite these contradictions. Today is CarneBall Bizarre, and the name means exactly what it sounds like: this is where people come to celebrate extravagance, in full knowledge that normality is an illusion.

The club hosts a series of explicitly queer events, the best known of which is probably the Gegenparty, which takes place once every couple of weeks. *Gegen* in German means to be against something, but *zugegen sein* situates this opposition in time. The *Gegenbewegung*, or counter-movement, is queerness, and queer sounds like the German word *quer*, which can

mean to go against something: against the norms of being white, heterosexual, living in Berlin with your small family in Prenzlauer Berg, going to bed at 10 p.m. so you can be at your best for your job the next morning. It means living out a different idea of what your life could be. Several years ago the market charged in and embarked on the commercialisation of subculture; well-known labels, from H&M to Louis Vuitton, designed gender-neutral lines of clothing, for example. So what happens when someone who is purportedly going against the grain looks just like you? Queerness also means to refashion oneself constantly, in order to be able to remain against the grain, 'a broken mirror that reflects one's own impossibilities', as the club's website says.

This is the abstract notion behind all these parties, but in reality queer people and their party culture have a new political opponent, one that sits in the German Parliament. In 2018 a Berlin representative of the AfD party wanted to close the

SOPHIE & TRIXI AT INSOMNIA BERLIN 8/11

the FEATHER BOA

world-famous Club Berghain and light up the darkrooms. The protests were fierce and loud, and the politician never introduced her bill. The opponent was visible, but the counter-movement was stronger.

Later that same year word shot through Berlin that a case of meningococcal meningitis had been detected at the club. A press release advised all guests to be examined and seek preventive care, as meningitis is transmissible through the mouth and throat by bodily fluids. Such news doesn't sit well with the city's ongoing gentrification, its mass tourism and the Senate's new codes.

Famous clubs such as Bar 25 or Farbfernseher finally had to close, and quite a few others are under threat, notwithstanding that clubs in Berlin bring in some €200 million (c. $245 million) each year. According to one major Berlin newspaper, even the KitKat's new investor wants to change its use. Queerness and counter-culture are only tolerated if they obey the market. An anarchic case of meningitis doesn't fit in well with the Senate's new fire-safety regulations and noise-abatement ordinances. It doesn't fit in with the explosion of rents and people moving to the city who, with their complaints, are transforming this former island into a global centre with its freshly painted façades.

There is no room for any of that tonight – at this hour. I throw myself into the darkness. We are among ourselves, falling over one another. Tonight we build a sense of oneness out of our diversity. 🐋

The Evicted Generation

The writer Annett Gröschner was one of the many liberty-craving young East Berliners who, in the 1980s, moved into the run-down Prenzlauer Berg district, a refuge for artists, intellectuals and dissidents. After the fall of the Wall the local authorities, which owned most of the buildings, promised to restore them and keep the existing social fabric intact, but what actually happened was very different.

ANNETT GRÖSCHNER
Translated by Stephen Smithson

Left: The Wasserturm, a former water tower, is one of the iconic landmarks of Prenzlauer Berg. The building, in which people were once imprisoned and tortured by the Nazis, has now been converted into private apartments.

My Berlin begins on a summer's day in 1983. A clapped-out lorry with a Magdeburg licence plate drops a couple of cardboard boxes in a rear courtyard on Schönhauser Allee. The boxes are carried up to a first-floor flat – one of those poorly lit Berlin rooms with a kitchen and an outside toilet half a flight of stairs down, its floor completely rotten. The door to the flat has been left leaning against the wall, and the *Kachelofen* stove does not work – although I will not find this out until late in the autumn. But there is electricity and running water, and there's a public lavatory in the U-Bahn station opposite, which keeps longer hours than the local Kaufhalle supermarket. Serving as key to the flat is a hook that I have bent into shape – I always knew those compulsory practical classes at school would come in useful sometime somewhere – and have given it the name Dietrich, as lock-picks tend to be called in German. 'We live illegally – remind yourself every day that were this not so / we would both be out on the streets,' wrote the young poet Uwe Kolbe two streets to the east. My residence here is illegal but tolerated. Every month I transfer thirty East German marks (c. $2.50) in rent to an account with the KWV, the cooperative that administers local housing. It is said that once you have made three or more rent payments it becomes less easy for them to throw you out, unless you have chosen to occupy the wrong kind of flat – a Stasi safe house, for example, or part of the quota set aside for newly released prisoners.

This, then, is how I came to Berlin and stayed. In all the years since my arrival I've kept within a radius of little more than two kilometres from where I started out, and yet everything has changed fundamentally. For any young person who did not want to stagnate in the provinces in the early 1980s there were three legal options: Dresden, Leipzig and East Berlin. The last of these was the closest to me geographically – and in mentality, too. It's true that Dresden and Leipzig, like Berlin, had condemned parts where like-minded people lived and where it was possible to get by pretty well, but Saxony was not for me. The Prussian in me, of whom there was still a vestige, wanted the capital of Prussia – although the official status of the city to which I moved was that of the capital of the GDR, and there was nothing to suggest that this would ever change.

Ever since I'd seen Konrad Wolf's film *Solo Sunny* in 1980, about a misfit singer living in Prenzlauer Berg, I'd had a setting for my dream of independence: a flat with a large room on the fourth floor at the rear of a building overlooking a courtyard with a carpet-beating stand, three grey bins, cooing pigeons and every ten minutes a yellow-and-red S-Bahn briefly visible through the courtyard entrance as it passed by. There would be notes on the front door on which friends and acquaintances would leave messages for lack of a telephone, a large room with many books,

ANNETT GRÖSCHNER is an author and journalist. Founder and editor of several magazines, she has also worked for various newspapers, including *Frankfurter Allgemeine Zeitung*, *taz* and *Der Freitag*. She has collaborated with the Berlin theatres Maxim Gorki Theater, Theater an der Parkaue and Deutsches Theater and since 2015 has lectured in cultural journalism at the Berlin University of the Arts, having also worked at Humboldt University. She is the author of numerous books on the city of Berlin and on Prenzlauer Berg, the neighbourhood in which she has lived for almost forty years, and she also works at the local museum.

'The roofs of Prenzlauer Berg were a good place to be in those days. You stood above all the shitty conditions down below, close to the sky, and every few minutes a plane would fly over, only to land minutes later behind the Wall.'

a record player, tea in ceramic cups, a type-writer. Here I would be free.

My actual life in Berlin was damp, dark and devoid of the S-Bahn. The back of my building looked over the bottled-beer plant of the Schultheiss brewery – which, by that time no longer in operation, was just a tangle of labyrinthine underground passages. No brewing had taken place there for a long time, the practice having been abandoned just like everything else in this place. Even the cemeteries no longer saw any burials. I had come into a society in stasis – 'decline' would be too suggestive of activity – or what the poet Elke Erb called 'a compactly enclosing stagnation'. The blinds in the ground-floor apartments were always closed, and there were just one or two corner premises with *Kneipen* that operated like extended living rooms. Without these bars socialism would have been even less bearable, but still I felt at home here imme-diately – just as six years later Kreuzberg in the West would feel as familiar as if I had never been anywhere else and the Wall had been no more than a concrete fart. For all I knew back then in 1983, however, the Wall was there to stay – and there I was, scarcely two hundred metres away, my rope ladder made of thoughts.

There is a photo, taken in the 1970s by Helga Paris, of a Prenzlauer Berg street, old people shuffling along wide paths paved with the granite slabs known here as 'pork bellies', cars by the kerbside, the façades of the *Gründerzeit* houses grey, the sky grey, the coats of people and the street signs also grey. Despite a light coming from the south

a fog hangs over the road, the thought of which still makes me shiver. In my mind this is how it always seemed to be from October to April. The smell comes to my nose immediately – a mixture of coal, two-stroke mix, piss and stagnant water. The toilets would freeze in winter, and soot from the coal stoves would settle on the fabric in fine particles if you attempted to dry your laundry outside. But one thing in the photo is alive and unmistakable – a bird, its wings outstretched, grey like everything else but in mid-flight and coming towards the viewer.

Was there ever summer in the city? Yes. I remember a light glistening over completely empty streets, eight lanes all to oneself, as if no one else were around. In areas on the other side of the arterial road the war was still a presence. The façades were pocked with bullet holes marking the course of events in April 1945 when the battle was fought from house to house. The horror could be hidden under every grass patch, under every sealed surface, because when the rubble was being cleared away it had just been piled into the cellars. The filmmaker Jörg Foth wrote that whenever you rounded the corner in Prenzlauer Berg that corner was missing.

In the provinces of the GDR the saying 'city air makes you free' had a very special meaning. It actually dates from the Middle Ages, when a serf who could no longer tolerate his situation might settle in a city where he would be for the most part untraceable by the lord of the manor. Thus the legal tradition arose that a person

The long tradition of squatting in West Berlin hit its high point in 1981, when more than one hundred buildings were occupied in this way. In a few hours, simply by word of mouth, two thousand people could be mustered to prevent an eviction. There were many squatted apartments in East Berlin, too, but the squatters kept a low profile and made no political claims. That situation changed with the fall of the Wall and the anarchy that ensued. In early 1990 there were already seventy squats, and by that summer 128; now the youth of the East flew banners from the windows and recited their slogans. It has been estimated that there were more than twenty-five thousand empty apartments in East Berlin by then, many abandoned in haste by citizens fleeing the GDR via Hungary in the autumn of 1989, others awaiting demolition to make room for new, prefabricated structures. This was the case with the series of buildings on Mainzer Strasse in Friedrichshain that were squatted in May 1990. The occupants refused an initial compromise and pursued a strategy of escalation that forced the city to desist in their efforts to evict them, but on 14 November 1990, after days spent building barricades, police and squatters engaged in a veritable urban battle – stones and Molotov cocktails rained down from the windows on the police. The housing emergency is much worse now, but aside from some resistance around squatted houses on Rigaer Strasse and in Friedrichshain, the city has lost this revolutionary spirit.

living in a city could no longer be reclaimed by any master after a year and day and would thus become a free citizen.

When I moved to Berlin I, too, came a little closer to my idea of freedom. The Stasi found me a month later and took me to the police headquarters on Alexanderplatz for questioning. Even in the bewildering back-streets of Prenzlauer Berg one could not truly hide. I nevertheless felt at home here among those like-minded people – people who put on performances, wrote poems, made earrings or counterfeit goods, who were either waiting to leave for West Berlin and a life there that they imagined as one long Kreuzberg party or who wanted to stay because they still had an account open with the country in which they lived. Even East Berlin displayed the kind of tolerance that could easily be taken for indifference; anonymity was necessary to endure the excessive stimulation that came with life in a big city, even a big city in stasis.

I spent the turn of the year 1988–9 on a roof. The roofs of Prenzlauer Berg were a good place to be in those days. You stood above all the shitty conditions down below, close to the sky, and every few minutes a plane would fly over, only to land minutes later behind the Wall in another world. I once dreamed that I had managed to board one of those planes, but just before Tegel it crashed, and I sat with all the other passengers on a hill next to the wreckage and knew in my dream that it was still Prenzlauer Berg. Still East. Today planes land at the new Berlin Brandenburg Airport in Schönefeld. Where once we hung out our laundry to dry there are expensive attic apartments. You can't get up to the roofs any longer; the passages up to the flats are now cordoned off with barbed wire to keep burglars out. But when we spoke of freedom it was a different kind of freedom we had in mind – one that had nothing to do with property. It was slippery on the roof because the evening of 31 December 1988 was a cold one. Minutes into the new year four people fell from a nearby house along with the rubble of what had been a crumbling balcony. One of them died, and the others were seriously injured. It wasn't a good start to the year, but there was nothing about the incident that came as a surprise. We lived in a run-down place. Most of the balconies were closed off, but they were used anyway – to grow weed when light conditions allowed or for tests of courage. On some roofs there were holes as wide as the shoulders of coal-bearers, and the ladders to the skylights only had around half their rungs.

I don't remember what we wished for on the roof that New Year's Eve. None of us suspected that the coming year would change almost everything. To have predicted that the Wall would fall so quickly and bloodlessly and in such a relatively straightforward manner would have involved a leap of the imagination of which none of us was capable. We had, it was true, heard it rumoured that the GDR was bankrupt, but hadn't it always been that way, right from the start? We also didn't know how the changed situation would divide us.

Twenty days later my son came into the world. Seven weeks early. A bird fallen from its nest who could fit into your cupped hands, and, before anything else could happen, he needed to be nursed to health. Between us was a pane of glass. Outside snow fell.

In the early summer of 1989 I rode around the block with the child and asked myself, 'Who can say for sure that they won't start shooting here, too – just as they did at Tiananmen Square in Beijing?' Two months later several people in my area locked their flats, threw the keys into the river Spree and went through the hole in the fence to the West without looking back. Then events spiralled. I experienced the days between 7 October and 9 November 1989 as if intoxicated. At last something was happening. And the child was still here.

I wasn't happy the day the Wall came down. It's hard to explain today, but I suspected that from that point on there would be less focus on democracy and more on consumption. And while we were still holding anarchist-style birthday celebrations, the new GDR privatisation authority, the Treuhandanstalt, was acting behind our backs, flogging the silverware and disposing of the rest. Perhaps this is one reason why the upheaval was so peaceful – because there was nothing worth defending.

The 1990s were a transition period, bringing the return of many who had left Prenzlauer Berg for the West in the years before the Wall came down and the emigration of others who had until then remained. Some changed jobs. One made it into property speculation with an office on Kurfürstendamm. Others finally embarked upon that programme of study that had been denied them during the GDR era.

One-time drinking buddies and fellow culture workers started to find themselves on opposite sides of a desk – one a district councillor for social affairs, perhaps, while the other was applying for social assistance. 'Desperate social authorities took special measures to introduce the majority of unemployed poets and other art parasites into work simulation,' wrote Guillaume Paoli in a volume of essays to mark the passing of the *Sklavenmarkt* ('Slave Market') series of performances and events held 'in the lower abdomen of Berlin' between 1996 and 2000. If the day job in art or literature came to nothing – too many compromises involved – you could still open a bar and hold forth from either side of the counter against capitalism and its high culture, armed with beer against the youth who thirsted increasingly for mixed, shaken and stirred drinks. It was a productive decade for literature and the other arts. It is interesting that during the twenty years after the events of 1989 so many women, always under-represented within the scene's inner circle, stepped out of the shadows into the world: Cornelia Schleime in painting and Elke Erb in poetry, but also photographers such as Helga Paris, Maria Sewcz or Tina Bara, to name just a few.

Up to the mid-1990s there were few ways – certainly none of them financial – in which the people who came to Prenzlauer Berg, primarily from West Germany but also from all over the world, differed from the artists who were already living there before the fall of the Wall. They were people who wanted to give themselves a chance to experiment, attracted here, as others had been ten years earlier, by a supply of cheap accommodation and the chance to live among like-minded people. The question 'Where are you from?' therefore played only a very marginal role for all except those who wanted to exploit their East- or West-German life stories for ideological ends.

The availability of accommodation became increasingly squeezed once the principle of 'restitution before compensation' was enforced in Prenzlauer Berg and elsewhere. There followed a spate of 'warm renovations' – arson attacks, often undetectable, for the purposes of insurance fraud. Prenzlauer Berg was turned into the largest construction site after Potsdamer Platz, and cheap, hard-to-heat dumps with outside toilets became a rarity. The renovations marked the beginning of what, with the harmless-sounding term *Abgeschlossenheitsbescheinigung* (certificate of completion), led to the flats within the blocks being sold off individually. That changed everything for the Prenzlauer Berg scene, which was sucked up into the vortex of a large-scale population exchange, suffering what might from an outside perspective be viewed as collateral damage.

The area's cultural decline coincides with the tendency to refer to it as 'Prenzlberg', a practice whose origins are unclear; the 'dream in strawberry foliage' – as the German title of *Comrade Couture* (*Ein Traum in Erdbeerfolie*), Marco Wilms's 2009 film about the underground fashion scene in Prenzlauer Berg, translates – vanished into thin air. Prenzlberg was cute, and what is cute loses the power to unsettle. For the high-income bourgeoisie, mostly from the inheritance generation, it became fashionable to buy a flat in Prenzlauer Berg instead of a home on the edge of the city. Location, location, location was now the guiding principle. The word that Prenzlauer Berg was now domesticated spread far and wide. Meanwhile, cultural institutions were dismantled and funds cut as the financial crisis of 2008 started a capital flight into property – since which time the displacement of those on low incomes has intensified, affecting most artists and writers.

Structurally Kreuzberg, which was on the western side of the Wall, is the most obvious point of comparison with Prenzlauer Berg. In much the same way it drew young people with pacifist inclinations from the provinces to settle and rescue houses earmarked for demolition and to create a culture of their own. For many years two features protected Kreuzberg from change beyond recognition: a population of Turkish and Arab origin and a low availability of property for private ownership. Prenzlauer Berg did not enjoy the same kind of population diversity, particularly since every flat conversion caused the area, and possibly the city, to lose at least one tenant born and raised in the GDR together with their children. In consequence, the children of the well-heeled are now among their own kind in nurseries and primary schools. Nowhere do teachers get to feel their loss of status so keenly as in a Prenzlauer Berg primary school. Now, however, Kreuzberg, too, is being bought up.

With a short break I have lived in Prenzlauer Berg for thirty-eight years, fifteen of which I have spent as a freelance writer on the edge of Friedrichshain park. My flat has always been my workplace, and here I keep my archive and my library. I moved in 2000, not voluntarily but – like almost everyone in the area – to make way for property renovation. We were supposed to be happy about the new bathrooms, the balconies and the bright façades. And happy we were. After all, we had been here before the Wall came down, and it had been our readiness at that time to live in apartments lacking in creature comforts that had prevented these dilapidated old buildings from collapsing, rotting or being burned down.

Until a few years ago this part of the city held the status of a redevelopment area, which was supposed to protect it from social segregation and the displacement of long-term, low-income residents. But this protection was not afforded – quite the opposite. Tenants were tolerated up to, but not beyond, the point at which the most

profitable marketing was possible. Because most buildings were given certificates of completion at the time of renovation, each flat could be sold individually into private ownership. The agreement I had regarding the 'final conversion' was with a limited company called Pluton. I asked myself at the time whether it was cynicism or stupidity that led to a property company being named after the ancient god of the underworld – and that question has since been answered.

In 2010 I learned that my flat had been sold to an individual in 2002 without my knowledge. Correct procedure had not been followed: the flat should have been offered to me first. However, the statute of limitations now applied. Until then, the word *Eigenbedarf* (required for personal use) was not part of my active vocabulary, although, unexpectedly, I managed to find it in the 1979 Leipzig edition of the Duden dictionary in a supplement dealing with tenancy law.

It started in 2010 with a phone call that didn't seem at the time to give me undue cause for concern. At the other end was a male voice that asked, in rather a brusque manner, if we could make an appointment for my flat to be measured up. 'You must have got the wrong number,' I said. 'I am acting on behalf of Deutsche Bank,' said the voice, a tad more disgruntled. 'So what?' I replied. 'That doesn't give you the right to enter my flat.' After some back and forth, in which disgruntlement gave way to anger, the voice promised, 'You will be hearing from me.' I hung up. A few minutes later the housing-association agent responsible

Above: The pedestrian bridge between Kopenhagener Strasse and Dänenstrasse, one of the few corners of Prenzlauer Berg that still retains the feel of the 1990s. The cellar of the Kohlenquelle, the bar to the left of the end of the bridge, was the venue for the illegal Mittwochsklub evenings.
Above right: The city's oldest *Biergarten*, the Prater, also famous for its theatre.

for my flat was on the phone, requesting that I please allow the surveyor into the flat; the owner wants to change his credit line, which means that the number of square metres must be established accurately. 'Which owner?' I asked. 'I believe you own the block of flats.' 'No,' said the agent, 'we are only the administrators. Your block is in co-ownership.'

Originally the whole building had belonged to the Bavaria. As the property subsidiary of Berlin's state banking group – in 2000 its letterhead read Bavaria Unternehmensgruppe Bankgesellschaft Berlin AG – the Bavaria had been caught

up in the Berlin banking scandal (see the sidebar on page 148). Most of us have already forgotten that the closed funds (or, in banking speak, innovative capital-investment products) with their promise of risk-free returns, invested for the self-proclaimed elite of the new capital and other profiteers, almost brought the city to bankruptcy. Taxpayers paid for the mess and are still paying for it. The effects of this selfish, acquisitive mentality can still be seen today – in a lack of housing, ineffective policing, poorly functioning public transport, overburdened public services and, after 2015, a scandal involving the treatment of refugees, a scandal that came about because there weren't even any computers on which to register them.

We – who in many cases had for decades been tenants of the houses in the redevelopment areas – may have enjoyed some benefits in the short term. Seen from a longer-term perspective, however, we were – and this did not become clear to me until later – nothing more than bodies manning the fort until the fully refurbished buildings could be profitably marketed. In an earlier period in Berlin's development, people fulfilling this function were referred to as 'dry dwellers'.

By the time of the surveyor's phone call I had been living in Prenzlauer Berg for almost thirty years. I had lived in properties of the municipal housing management and in the notorious Alscher houses, named after the company that managed the private properties of owners in the West. I had squatted flats and rented flats, I had felt the effects of the Unification Treaty with its slogan 'restitution before compensation' with the subsequent 'warm renovations' and the beginning of what – with the harmless-sounding term 'certificate of completion' – led to the flats being repurposed into small, compact homes and sold off to individual owners. Fewer than 20 per cent of those living in the Prenzlauer Berg redevelopment areas at the start of renovation are still there today. In the Winsviertel quarter of Prenzlauer Berg the proportion is just 16 per cent, only half of whom are still in the same flat. Measured against the original policy aim of renovating the area for the residents while maintaining the social structure, the programme must be judged a failure. Flats in the redevelopment areas should for the most part have been kept off the market. But the state government – although a coalition of the left and centre left that had been in power for years – failed to consider this. On the contrary, by demolishing the old prefabricated buildings – a move that now looks to have been unnecessary – it exacerbated the housing shortage and drove up rents.

During one panel discussion, the former managing director of a company that carries out cautious urban renewal asserted that after the fall of the Wall there had been no long-established population in Prenzlauer Berg which required protection from displacement; it had become a transit area for young people, and those with long-term housing needs were by that time living in areas with estates of prefabs. In translation this means that the priority task of socially acceptable urban renewal – that is, to protect low-income tenants from being displaced – had not even been deemed necessary in Prenzlauer Berg. With the help of a false assertion a failure of social urban renewal could be spun as a success: look how lovely it all looks again where the communists once allowed everything to fall into ruin.

Twenty years on and what was once a socially mixed area has become a largely homogeneous part of town – middle aged, middle class, middle educated but above middle income, because otherwise the rents would no longer be affordable or the loans serviceable. Tellingly, the only undertaker's in the area has had to close, its premises now taken over by a delicatessen.

Because the neighbourhood in which I lived was becoming increasingly popular and a demand was being created that led people, for reasons that weren't clear to me, to pay astronomical rents or to buy properties at inflated prices, the rental index as a whole was driven upwards. The upshot was that at the most recent prices the figure for the basic rent of my flat was as high as it had been when I moved in fifteen years earlier – only now the currency was euros not Deutschmarks. The rent had doubled, but the flat had not got any more comfortable or any lighter, airier or sunnier. It remained a north-facing apartment that tilted, preventing the doors from closing properly, which sometimes assisted invisible hands to open them during the night. The tilt had been caused in part by an unexploded shell that had ripped through the building during the Second World War and in part by the chain mines and high-explosive bombs that had also wiped out almost half the houses along the street.

I looked up the address of the owners of my flat on Google Street View and found

CITY FOR RENT

Berlin is a city of unlit apartments and empty buildings because its rents are too high. Even though 55 per cent of Berliners choose to rent instead of buying a property, the property market became monopolised in the 1990s by speculating companies that bought apartments and then resold them at a higher price. The strategy was designed to increase demand each year and to have a regular turnover of residents. Since the start of the 21st century Berlin has seen a price hike of 120 per cent in the property sector, and more than 200,000 apartments are in the hands of private financial groups. Berliners' patience has reached its limit. The Deutsche Wohnen & CO Enteignen initiative/movement is calling for a referendum proposing the expropriation of all properties from companies that own more than three thousand apartments. The cost of this measure would be €28–36 billion ($34–44 billion). The Berlin Senate has also made a move: in November 2020 it passed a law that puts a cap on rents (for houses built before 2014) for a period of five years. Where the actual rent exceeds the established ceiling by more than 20 per cent, the landlord is obliged to reduce it. Thanks partly to the pandemic rents fell immediately but so did the number of apartments on the market.

A few years after the Wall fell, a banking scandal on an unprecedented scale broke in Berlin, causing so much damage to the city's balance sheet that its taxpayers are still paying down the debt. In 1995 a holding company of various banks called the Bankgesellschaft Berlin (BgB) was formed, majority owned by the Region of Berlin. Using funds financed in part with public money, several BgB executives bought apartments in East Berlin (the infamous *Plattenbauten*, large apartment buildings made of prefabricated concrete slabs) and sold them to private investors, who included members of the CDU and SPD political parties. The funds had very favourable terms and conditions for the property market, meaning very competitive interest rates, terms of twenty-five to thirty years and the guarantee of reimbursement upon entry into the agreement. The dealings of Klaus-Rüdiger Landowsky, *éminence grise* of the Christian Democrat Party and manager of two of the banks involved (Hyp and Investitionsbank), and of some of his colleagues were declared illegal by investigators. Landowsky was sentenced to over a year in jail, although his imprisonment was suspended. In the meantime, the region's coffers had been depleted, and so the city asked the federal government to intervene, but then Chancellor Schröder refused his support. This resulted in the resignation of the mayor, Eberhard Diepgen, and the start of an austerity and widespread privatisation policy to fill the gaping hole in the city's budget.

a single-family home on the outskirts of the city. These people didn't need my flat, so they wouldn't try to register a requirement for personal use; if they did they would never get away with it. This thought reassured me to an extent, and I made an appointment with the surveyor. All was quiet for a while. I wrote a novel about an old woman cleared out of the flat in which she had lived for fifty years. The *Frankfurter Allgemeine Zeitung* asked in its review why I saw only the negative side of Berlin. The book didn't sell particularly well. I had to take on several jobs, so I would then work at my bay window until well into the night. I had friends who were happy to have me as their night light when they got home at three in the morning, because all the street had to offer were the old lamps from the days of the GDR. It was becoming harder with each month for me to pay the ever-increasing rent. When my child moved out I began to look for a lodger, but unexpectedly the owners refused to grant permission to sublet. I brought in a lawyer who, with one glance at the owners' letter, ascertained that they had no right to refuse me, but before she had even had time to draft a reply the telephone rang.

On the other end, and about to enter my flat and my life on this day in early February 2014, was an estate agent, whom we'll call Walter Kettler. Speaking in a highly affected manner, he told me that he had been authorised by the owners to carry out the sale of the flat in which I was living and that if I wished to remain in the apartment he would be looking to sell to a capital investor; I would, of course, be welcome to bid for the property myself. I asked about the price. He named a sum approaching the middle-six-figure range; I was consumed by an upper-six-figure fit of laughter.

I had over the years read enough documents relating to these buildings to know that nobody had ever paid such a high price for a flat in this area. The lawyer advised me that matters were now becoming more complicated and that I should obtain an extract from the land registry. From this I learned that on 31 August 2001 the property-management company Pluton Immobilien Verwaltungs GmbH & Co. had registered the partition of my flat in accordance with Section 8 of WEG (the property law relating to flats). For the new owners the notice of conveyance was entered into the register on 23 September 2002. At that point I had been living in the flat for two years. In failing to ask me whether I wouldn't like to buy the flat myself, the hellhounds had broken the law, but, as my lawyer informed me, the statute of limitations now applied. I had been allowed to move into a flat that it was known was to be sold.

I am a renter out of conviction, and it is the fact that Berlin is a city for renters that has always made it such a great place in which to live. I feel this way not just because of the obligations that property brings but also because of what acquiring property through credit does to people – it makes cowards of them. The fear of losing jobs or orders and then no longer being able to service their loans causes them to put up with anything – or worse, to use the fact that they own a property as a basis on which to make demands on the city and on their neighbours. As rates of property ownership increased, clubs, leafy trees, pubs, smoking corners and even playgrounds started to disappear from Prenzlauer Berg. The area has become a boring, snoring place that I would have left long ago if it weren't my home. This is not something that I could have prevented. It overtook me, just as it overtook everyone who hadn't already moved away or been displaced.

The lawyer informed me that I was obliged, provided certain requirements were met, to allow potential buyers access and that, despite the assurances I'd been given, I should not entertain any hopes about my position if the buyer should claim that they needed the property for personal use. She pointed out that, although there was a seven-year notice period, this would apply only in cases of partition following a first-time sale and not in cases like mine where the flat had already been in private ownership for some time. Then the normal statutory notice period would apply, which, contrary to what was stated in my rental agreement, was only nine months. She was actually a good lawyer, but the law favoured the buyer.

On 15 March my doorbell rang at ten minutes to midday. Walter Kettler conformed to almost every cliché one might associate with an estate agent, albeit in 1980s-stereotype kind of way. He turned up in a Mercedes, old but well maintained, the kind that in the 1980s would have been a marker of success but today, compared with the SUVs making up the majority of cars in my street, looked like a pimpmobile. Herr Kettler wore gold chains and a signet ring, was small and fat and sweated when he had to walk up two floors. That morning he had doused his face, neck and hands in so much aftershave that I had to fumigate the place after he'd gone before I was able to regain any sense of having dominion over my own home. He immediately complained that doing business in Prenzlauer Berg was not easy, what with the riff-raff on site, prices distorted and about to go into a bubble, or something like that, whereas the solid terraced part of the area was an honest business.

He told me he had received several phone calls from people who had heard the name Prenzlauer Berg, thought it had

> '**I am a renter out of conviction, and it is the fact that Berlin is a city for renters that has always made it such a great place in which to live.**'

a good ring to it and had a sense that their money would be safe here. I told him that as far as I was concerned he didn't have to sell the flat, but he replied with a sigh that he was doing it for the owners, whom he had known for a long time and who wanted to retire now. It later turned out that they were my age; I had fed them so well for all these years that they were now in need of rest. My anger grew, not so much at Herr Kettler as at how it could even be possible that the most intimate human space, the home, could be treated as a commodity.

I don't know. If someone had thrown me out of my flat in the GDR era, under section whichever of whatever law, I would have been able to call the ZDF current affairs programme *Kennzeichen D* in the West, and the show would no doubt have made a feature about how the inviolability of a person's home was being trampled underfoot in the GDR.

But I can't remember any cases like mine cropping up in the old days. Even if you hadn't paid the rent for a year you didn't get thrown out. You didn't have to allow the police and state security to enter your property; they had to gain access covertly. And now, twenty-five years on, people were being allowed to offend my dignity by trampling on my privacy and laying claim to it. The first time somebody stepped over my threshold it was like being groped. The tenant advisory service recommend that you make your flat as unappealing as possible during viewings by potential buyers. No tidying up or getting rid of cobwebs, barricades made of rubbish, blood seeping from the refrigerator ...

Between March and June a total of ten interested parties entered my life, often accompanied by their partners and always on a Saturday. My flat is not just where I live but also where I work. Everything I own is assembled there as though on an exhibition table. There were interested parties who didn't even say hello, others who were emphatically friendly, some who were embarrassed and there was one who gave me looks meant to tell me that his wife had forced him to come along. They went into every room, looked into every corner, asked questions that I answered half-heartedly or inaccurately, and they read my life from the walls. A couple with completely silent children told me they already had a flat in the area but that they had now come into an unexpected inheritance. He was somebody I had seen around the local area at night with a different woman holding him tight, and she was one of those women whose fear of becoming overweight leads to them running through the streets towards Volkspark Friedrichshain three times a week. In an effort to regain sovereignty over my home and my life I wrote small portraits of potential buyers in my diary. One with a child in her arms dropped her key and expected me to pick it up; one said that my rent was far too low and some 'fine-tuning' was certainly in order. One of them formulated with deliberation a sentence that suggested I was headed for a life of serfdom: 'I will then be your owner, and you will be my tenant.' And I wrote three pages about the pilot who said to my face in an unguarded moment, 'I can see the fear in your eyes.'

Over the next few weeks I suffered

outbursts of anger, nightmares and depression. I could no longer work or eat, and I saw myself being pushed out of the door.

In July the people described to me by the estate agent as 'saviours' came. They came across as busy in a globalised way, self-assured and with a chequebook-like friendliness, the kind of couple you see a thousand times jogging around these parts – water-drinkers to whom nothing ever sticks, people without qualities but with money, people who could be doing any job in middle management, selling guns, prostheses or property. The hope I expressed in my diary was muted. I didn't find them likeable, right from the point where they failed to look me in the eye. But likeability wasn't the issue. They already had a flat in Berlin but lived abroad, and they talked with the agent about the return my flat would bring them. In August I received the news that the couple without qualities had been declared successful bidders and the notice of conveyance had been entered in the land register.

In October I received in the mail a notice of termination through *Eigenbedarf*. The closing sentence informed me that they, the new owners, would unfortunately have to evict me because they had an urgent need to start a family and that would be possible only in my flat, since their other flat was too small and also rented out to a cousin without means. The lawyer described property owners wanting to start a family as the glue of capitalism. She held out no hope for me.

In the fifteen years that I lived in the flat I never felt that it was a subject I had to write about. Now that I've lost it that has changed. I have a recurring dream in which the flat is empty except for sheets of paper with the outline of my latest novel lining the walls of the study and a mattress with a bedsheet on it with me naked underneath.

The door opens, and the new owners enter. But I won't leave; I have no clothes to put on.

I now avoid the neighbourhood in which I lived for almost twenty years because every time I pass the lighted windows, with their curtains closed so that no one can see in, a cold anger grips me; it is pointless and unproductive. At such moments I think of the land-register extract in which the bank loan of the new owner is recorded, the six-figure sum and the possibility that the flat won't bring them any children.

I have been living north of the Ringbahn, Berlin's circular railway, for four years, still in Prenzlauer Berg but in a residential part designed in the 1920s as a counter-balance to the styles of the *Gründerzeit*. The homes are small, low-rise blocks. The residents are mixed: there are old people who have lived here since the 1950s and there are younger people who live off welfare and very young people starting a family. Cars seem to get smaller when they cross the bridge from the city centre, and the push-chairs and bicycles cheaper. As long as I can pay the rent, I'll stay here.

Today's Prenzlauer Berg with its stock of *Gründerzeit* housing is no longer inhabitable as a real place for autonomous art – for now. One could wait until the clinker bricks fall from the façades and rats, birds and foxes have eaten their way through the Styrofoam that veneers and insulates the old, eroded façades. Then maybe there will be free spaces again. But, as the painter Gerd Hillich said in 1999, 'At some point the stage has been reached where the myth has found its fixed form and will survive for thousands of years. Prenzlauer Berg does not actually need to have existed; the myth is enough. It should be encouraged. The spirit hovers over it, and there the matter is settled.' ✒

East vs. East

The destinies of the two former East Berlin football teams BFC Dynamo and FC Union have always been intertwined: BFC once dominated the GDR championships but now languishes in the lower regional divisions, while Union has been promoted to the top-flight Bundesliga. These are two clubs with complex identities caught between the past and the future.

ALINA SCHWERMER
Translated by Stephen Smithson

Left: Diehard BFC Dynamo fan Dirk on the terraces at the Berlin team's former home ground, the Friedrich-Ludwig-Jahn-Sportpark.

Berlin is not considered a football city by the people who live there, and yet it has several clubs, many with quite distinctive fan bases. Hertha BSC is the big western club, polarising, decried as arrogant, forever looking out for its own interests, but there are smaller neighbourhood clubs with relatively large followings, such as the left-wing Tennis Borussia Berlin or the Turkish-migrant outfit Türkiyemspor Berlin, long renowned for its integration work. And then, of course, there are the two clubs of the former German Democratic Republic – the former Oberliga champions BFC Dynamo, now fallen low, and Union Berlin, now in the Bundesliga.

Union's tranquil, rural-seeming setting is a key part of its brand – and it's even become something of a cliché. Visitors to home fixtures at this top-division team, rather than having to cross the usual wastelands of car parks and muddy, trampled grass, find themselves walking through a small woodland glade of a kind that might be expected to lead to a family holiday resort or an enchanted never-never land. On a normal day at Union's Alte Försterei (Old Forestry) stadium one is struck by the overwhelming quiet. It's a scene that comes alive on match days only. Nobody on the paths, sprinklers on the pitch and the secretary in the office chatting with the postman.

Home games, however, have regularly attracted a crowd of twenty-two thousand – and the stadium is now being expanded to hold thirty-seven thousand. The crowd still comes mostly from Köpenick, the Berlin borough in which Alte Försterei is situated, and it's here that the tram to the ground starts to fill up on match days with people speaking in heavy Berlin accents. Nevertheless, these days you'll hear every hipster talking about how absolutely *super* Union is, and there have even been reports in *Der Tagesspiegel* of Brits flying in. Yes, it's a bit different here – sufficiently so for that difference to be a selling point.

Now Union Berlin has reached the top, winning promotion to the Bundesliga – the promised land traditionally inhabited by seventeen western teams plus RB Leipzig, which was created by Red Bull as a marketing vehicle. In the multi-million-dollar business of football, where so much is cruder and more obvious than in real life, the public was touched by this tale of success for a team from the ex-communist eastern part of Germany – but, of course, the persistence of the 'East' label thirty years on from the fall of the Wall is a source of irritation.

Meanwhile, not far from Alte Försterei, BFC Dynamo has just avoided relegation to a fifth-tier regional league. The one-time GDR Oberliga champion has fallen so low that its dilapidated Friedrich-Ludwig-Jahn-Sportpark gives the impression of being some kind of throwback to a more primitive time in otherwise spruced-up Prenzlauer Berg. In fact, so dilapidated is

ALINA SCHWERMER studied journalism and is currently responsible for the sports section of *taz*; she also writes for the weekly *Jungle World*. Born in Cologne and a Bayern Munich fan, she is a Berliner by adoption.

the iconic GDR-era stadium that it has now been slated for demolition and the team obliged to return to their historic home, the Sportforum in Hohenschönhausen. The story of the old arch-enemies BFC and Union could be recast as a Shakespearean drama: two Berlin football clubs, not quite alike in dignity, in ancient grudge united. But, in real life, the tale has many shades of grey.

WHAT DOES 'THE EAST' MEAN FOR FANS TODAY?

In the GDR BFC Dynamo was known as the Stasi club because it was the favourite team of state security minister Erich Mielke, who became its honorary chairman. Almost all GDR clubs had affiliations; BFC's just happened to be with the organ of state security. Union Berlin, in contrast, was a club with a civic mission: it was there to entertain the workers and not be too successful. Union's predecessor, SC Union Oberschöneweide, defined itself early on as a club for the working class, and in the 1920s the players mostly came from working-class backgrounds. This aspect of the club's history is recalled at the stadium today in a prologue to the club anthem that tells of the *Schlosserjungs*, or metalworker boys, as the players used to be known, and the legendary match with Hertha BSC when the now famous 'Eisern Union' ('Iron Union') chant reportedly first rang out. To this day Union followers use '*eisern*' as a greeting and valediction, and intellectuals like to idealise their underdog image.

BFC Dynamo, for its part, was able to call upon the refereeing industry for friendly support in the early 1980s, helping it to repeated championship wins. But since German reunification the club has fallen low, while Union – a popular club in the GDR era but mostly in the lower regions of the old Oberliga – is now, after a long period of turmoil after 1990, bringing in money and attaining cult status. How and why did it all turn out like this, and what does 'the East' mean to fans today?

Football history tells the history of Germany – specifically, in this case, that of the traces left by the GDR years. When the post-communist so-called 'turnaround' happened Rolf Walter thought it was 'cool' – the sixty-year-old uses this word today. 'I always wanted the change to come.' At the time Walter was active in opposition groups within the Protestant Church-based peace movement, including the Kirche von Unten and the Friedrichsfelde peace circle, and for this activity he turned down a permit to move abroad in 1988. Today Walter works as a freelance photographer, but at the beginning of the 1980s he was still a signalman for Deutsche Reichsbahn, the GDR railway, in Berlin. He experienced his first taste of rebellion at BFC Dynamo, the Stasi club. Anyone who thinks it might be difficult to get fans to talk about football under a dictatorship is wrong. Walter talks about it thoughtfully and with humour, as though he'd been waiting for someone to ask.

A PROVOCATIVE STUNT

Today BFC supporters are associated mostly with the political right, but in the early 1980s they were a more diverse group. 'The BFC following was actually a curious mixture of subcultures,' remembers Walter: punks, skinheads and various hard-to-define mutations and hybrids. Walter came to BFC by chance through his grandfather, a staunch comrade, at a time when there was even a small newspaper kiosk at the stadium that would lend pennants to fans to wave and show their support. The rowdier youth element started to follow the club at the beginning of the 1980s.

'There was a lot of messing about on

away trips, and only then did you get to feel your own power. When we went up against a thousand Union supporters with just two hundred of us we realised that if we stuck together we'd have a crazy amount of power.' Walter joined in with the fighting back then. At that time none of this was politically motivated, he says; these were provocative stunts, a bit of a laugh. In Dresden, for example, they poked fun at the food shortage by taking along green bananas to throw at the opposing fans, shouting, 'We have brought you something – bananas, bananas.'

They set up a fan club for footballer Lutz Eigendorf, who fled the GDR and was possibly murdered by the Stasi. It survived until the Stasi seized the fan-club flag. On away trips they would hear punk bands and music from the West, or a man with purple hair might yell 'Free love!', and people would keep their children off the streets. 'The Stasi were relatively reserved in their reaction to us because they were happy to see that BFC had supporters. In the mid-1980s that changed because they realised they were losing control, but by then things had really got out of hand,' says Walter. 'The more violence they used the more they radicalised the people.'

Both the club itself and the western-German press missed a trick in not ensuring that the more complex aspects of BFC history were passed down to the present. After reunification BFC came to be seen as simply the embodiment of the system, an absurd situation when this same system had financed almost all clubs and not just BFC. Still, BFC became stuck with its image as the club with far-right and hard-line-communist associations. A once wildly diverse following took a uniform turn to the right, a move hastened by harsh prison sentences, a growing thug contingent and the allure of being provocative

– from punk to neo-Nazi was not such a leap. BFC supporters, fighting and looting amid the anarchy of the post-reunification period, made the *Wessis* shudder. Their once-subversive humour was forgotten, and the story of the good rebels became that of Union.

In 1984 Walter was one of those who ended up in jail; when he got out he committed himself to political resistance. 'If I have to go back inside I'll do it properly, by being part of the opposition.' These days he will attend the odd BFC match, at which you can still see a GDR flag hanging in the crowd. For many this is just a way of being provocative, he feels. 'I don't think this is *Ostalgie* [nostalgia for *Ostdeutschland*]. Quite a few ended up in jail during the GDR era. The East German spirit is stronger at Union; they mourn for the past much more there,' says Walter. But is that true? It is one of the inconsistencies of this story that each side believes the other to be more inveterately *Ossi*.

A CLUB PROTECTED BY THE SYSTEM

When the so-called turnaround came, Lopez did not want East Germany to join with the West in the Federal Republic. 'As a GDR citizen I was never one of those who wanted to run away,' he says today. 'In principle I found socialism good, but I was aware that something was going wrong in the East.' Lopez has been a Union supporter since 1977 and came to the stadium for the first time when he was twelve. He is a good-humoured, warm-hearted guy. He remembers a young, rebellious crowd, most of them under the age of twenty-five. The satirical paper *Eulenspiegel* later proposed that 'Not every Union supporter is an enemy of the state, but every enemy of the state is a Union supporter,' which became a popular saying among Union fans. 'There is some truth to it,' believes Lopez. Götz, then groundsman at Union, also dreamed of a third way between socialism and capitalism that would follow communism. In retrospect, he thinks it was very naive. 'But everything seemed possible when the Wall came down.' This was very briefly true for the clubs in the East, too.

Union Berlin, which developed from FC Olympia Oberschöneweide, founded in 1906, cultivated its image as a workers' club rooted in the people from its earliest days. How much dissident activity there was among its supporters can hardly be quantified for sure today. According to historian Jutta Braun from sports-history centre Zentrum deutsche Sportgeschichte, many opposition contacts among Union fans can be found in Stasi files.

Of course, the club was still protected by the system, and every Union president was a party member. One area of major difference between Union and BFC, however, is in their treatment of GDR symbols. Lopez remembers how as a protest in 1990 he wore a small GDR badge at an away game. 'I was stopped immediately by other Union fans saying, "Get that shit off."' Götz remembers a pub in Köpenick that had Union and GDR insignia in the window a few years ago. Fans said, 'They do not belong together.'

SUFFICIENT DISTANCE FROM THE GDR

The question arises today, why Union? Good fortune and happy circumstance play a part in the answer: a broad base, local support and a demonstrable distance from the old system, which makes it compatible with the values of the West. Furthermore, a publicly visible Nazi problem does not exist and never has existed at Union, because, as Götz puts it, 'You leave your political ideas behind when you go through the turnstiles.' No GDR flags, no Nazi banners and any disputes are resolved within the family.

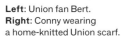

This sounds more like *The Godfather* than the left-wing following of Hamburg club FC St Pauli with which Union Berlin is often compared.

The reunification of the two German football systems took place in 1990, and the experience here in many ways reflects what was happening in other areas of German life after the fall of communism. It was a process that had little to do with equal treatment. Only two teams from the East were admitted to the new Bundesliga; this was the compromise between the DFB (the German Football Association) and NOFV (North-East German Football Association), its new regional association in the territories of the former GDR. And with four teams relegated at the end of the season (instead of the usual two) the sorting process was complete. The second-tier 2. Bundesliga admitted six clubs from the East. The representatives of East German football had wanted to secure a place in one of the first two divisions of the new Bundesliga for each of their fourteen top-division clubs, and their failure to do this had serious consequences.

Both BFC and Union failed to qualify for professional football. Caught between collapsing structures, players migrating to the West, ailing infrastructure and a new market economy, the eastern clubs faltered – many never to recover. In the medium term the most successful have been the clubs that were once rather insignificant, such as Hansa Rostock or Energie Cottbus – and finally, after years of decline, Union, too.

Götz is convinced that every team has a kind of DNA, something that withstands all external events. 'Despite all the mismanagement scandals in the early years in the new Germany, Union never lost the image of actually being the cool club.' Creative fan-based campaigns have time and again saved the club both directly and indirectly from bankruptcy – the Save Union demonstration at the Brandenburg Gate, the Bleed for Union blood-donor campaign or the renovation of the stadium by volunteers – and these at some point became a factor in marketing the club nationally. Is one of the reasons for Union's success that the club has managed to associate the East not with the GDR but with values of closeness and solidarity?

'*Ostalgie* doesn't play any role for us,' says Lopez firmly, not even in the club's public image. This is a point stressed by many Union supporters, who add that some of the lyrics to 'Eisern Union' – the club chant famously covered by Nina Hagen in which Union celebrates itself as 'we from the East [who] march forever ahead' and who 'won't let ourselves be bought by

Berlin? The media label of 'East-German club' is completely outdated; identity is purely regional, say many.

A MASS OF CONTRADICTIONS

The collapse of the communist system in East Germany came as a disaster for Janusz Berthold, then fifteen years old. Berthold's first conscious memory of BFC Dynamo's former stadium dates back to 1984, and he was brought up in accordance with the party line. He comes from a communist family, his grandfather in the anti-fascist resistance, his father in the Ministry for State Security. 'The fall of the Wall came as the greatest blow possible to our ideals,' he says, and he believes that his father and grandfather were destroyed as a result.

Janusz himself was planning a future in foreign espionage at the HVA, the GDR's foreign intelligence service. To this day he remains a convinced Marxist, and yet he says, 'I am now glad that it didn't go on as it was. Realistically, the GDR no longer had a future.' Berthold is not one of those people you would automatically associate with BFC. As someone who goes to alternative bars and left-wing demos and at the same time uses Berlin dialect even for emails, he would be placed somewhere between Union and a left-leaning amateur club. In some ways BFC Dynamo remains a mess of contradictions.

In the wild 1990s Berthold stopped supporting BFC because there was little room there for leftists. Instead, he sought to join AFFI, the anti-fascist fan initiative. But in 1999 he was one of the fans who came back to BFC. He divides BFC's post-communist history into periods: first came the time of the Stasi stigma; then the hooligan and fascist era; then in 2001 the club, briefly renamed FC Berlin, filed for insolvency and dropped as far as the tier-six Verbandsliga.

the West' – are not to the taste of many of its supporters. It is indeed true that there are lively arguments in the online Union Forum as to whether fans should sing along to the lines at all. Some call the sentiments idiotic, backward-looking and plain wrong because, ironically, it was a rich westerner who saved the club in 1998. And yet people roar along at the tops of their voices when the anthem is played in the stadium, the East and rebellion suddenly becoming bedfellows. 'Large parts of the fan base don't see themselves as part of an eastern club anyway, because as a Berliner you felt superior to the *Zonis* (inhabitants of the former Soviet Occupation Zone) in GDR times,' says Götz. Lopez recalls how, with GDR flags in many away stadiums after the fall of the Wall, Union fans made fun of the provincial idiots. Not so dissimilar, then, from the attitude of 'There's Berlin, and the rest is a village' that led BFC fans to throw bananas in Dresden. What does talk of East and West matter to people from

DIRK ZINGLER'S STASI PAST

BFC Dynamo has always been tagged as the Stasi team, but the biggest Stasi-related scandal was associated with the president of Union, Dirk Zingler, who ended up in the public eye in 2011 when journalist Matthias Wolf revealed that Zingler had been a member of the Feliks Dzerzhinsky Guards Regiment, the paramilitary wing of the Stasi. The Union president had, in fact, attained the rank of non-commissioned officer, but he had always omitted this dark paragraph from his biography. Just a few years earlier the team had parted ways with a sponsor for its past relationship with the Stasi. On this occasion, though, the club turned on Wolf, the *Wessi* who had wagged his finger at the East. Union's representatives refused to respond to his questions at press conferences, adopting a defensive position of 'We the East'; Union emphasised this standoff by saying that Wolf had made too much of a teenager's guard duty. Zingler today says that, yes, he can be morally judged for his service at the time, 'but the persons with the greatest standing to judge my life in the GDR are those who lived there. There are many who suffered greatly at the hands of the Stasi. When they say that the subject is taboo, they have my greatest understanding. I, too, condemn the crimes that were committed in the GDR.' The scandal did not bring him down, and Union's image was not tarnished in the process either.

UNION – ON THE RISE SINCE 2008

It is now the stuff of legend how BFC became caught up in a web of associations with right-wing hooligans, rockers and organised crime; a leading member of the Hells Angels now sits on the club's board. 'Until ten years ago it was hard to get away from the past. Since then the Stasi thing has started to slip into the background. The problem lies with right-wing extremist ideas, and the club has never gone far enough in clearly distancing itself from those.' There is not much room to manoeuvre if you don't want to drive away the old fans and you've no fresh wind blowing in from outside – not that it would be welcome anyway.

Yet something has changed. Nazi insignia has not been seen on BFC's terraces for a long time. The last major violent incidents were in 2011. All the talk is of how much effort the club's management is putting into attempts to improve its image. The club is looking for a new start. 'A lot of people who come to the ground are the old fans,' says Berthold, 'many of whom have now ended up in the [far-right, anti-Islam] Pegida movement. At the same time there is the youth-team substructure with a lot of migrant children. That's the bizarre thing about the club.' Furthermore, BFC is unusual among clubs with right-wing fan bases in not having a strong following among the young. This is probably because the club is now something of an irrelevance within the game.

Despite everything, many in eastern Germany are generous in their assessment of the terms of football unification. The historian Jutta Braun says that the process was carried out with such haste only at the urging of NOFV, which saw that its structures were collapsing. There wasn't much wiggle room. 'I wouldn't blame that on the West,' says Braun. Nonetheless, she adds that the commercialisation of football in the mid-1990s, coming after this change, dealt a second tragic blow to the game in the East.

Since winning promotion to the second division in the 2008–9 season, Union Berlin has essentially known just one direction: up. Never has it attracted such large crowds, never has it been so hyped nationwide – praised for its terraces, its atmosphere and its discerning approach to business. Nostalgia, yes, but not for the East. Promotion to the Bundesliga has been the club's stated goal for some years now, although not everyone connected with the club is enthusiastic about this. The main driver is Dirk Zingler, club president since 2004 and a self-described Union fan since childhood. Zingler receives you in his office directly opposite the Alte Försterei – a spacious room with a generous corner sofa. Zingler smokes in the office – a habit that makes him seem almost old-fashioned.

'Our identity as an eastern German club does not play a special role for us, but our identity more generally is important,' says Zingler immediately. To come from the eastern part of the city unfortunately still has political significance for some. 'For me, our political origins, the nature of the state system that produced us, does not matter. But regional affiliation is for me the core of the bond with a football club.' Regionalism is the big story for Dirk Zingler, and it's a story that he trots out as a matter of routine, one that he talks about constantly. Football for him is a regional business, and the club's experience in the period following reunification possibly helped to shape this view. 'Many things in the ex-GDR started to be controlled from outside after the fall of the Berlin Wall. Managers came over at the time and told us how the new state system was supposed to work. We stood

before them with our mouths agape. But the more time passed, the more we came to believe that, really, we just needed to look after ourselves. And the more a club does that, the better it gets on.'

Of course, its proximity to its home base is not the only explanation for Union's success, and a construct such as RB Leipzig demonstrates that a club can be successful without any roots. The Union promise is rather, 'You, too, can be a Köpenicker, my friend.' Like others, Zingler is painfully guarded when it comes to broaching the subject of the 'Ostklub thing' in conversation. He shows no wish to complain about the lack of integration of the eastern clubs after the fall of the Wall, and he says of the past, 'Of course, you can't deny your origins; the GDR era belongs to us. But it's only part of the story, and that story develops with every generation.'

This sense of an unfolding tale is an advantage not shared by BFC Dynamo, that state construct whose success was confined to the GDR years. For Union Berlin that time can seem like a past that's gradually being overwritten – nothing more than two blinks of an eye in a club history that began with a forerunner founded fifty years before the communist state came into being and that is now doing fantastically well thirty years after that state's demise – for the most part, at least.

BFC AND THE IMAGE QUESTION

Berliner Morgenpost statistics from a little while back suggest that Berlin remains a divided city when it comes to football. The figures showed that people from western districts are more likely to support Hertha, while those from the east of the city gravitate towards Union. This division need not be seen as political; there are also local traditions to consider, and Hertha has many supporters in the suburbs.

NINA HAGEN

Nina Hagen, the 'Godmother of Punk' – that's the title of the 2011 film dedicated to her – was born in East Berlin in 1955. She already had a career as a singer in the GDR – being known there for a single she recorded with her band Automobil, 'Du hast den Farbfilm vergessen' ('You Forgot the Colour Film'), a subtle satire on the drabness of the country at the time – before leaving East Germany to join her stepfather Wolf Biermann, a dissident musician who had been refused re-entry to the GDR following a tour of West Germany. After spending some time in London around the nascent late-1970s punk scene she returned to the FRG. There she put together the Nina Hagen Band along with members of the prog-rock act Locomotive Kreuzberg, and her new career in the West started to take off. In making full use of her distinctive six-octave-range operatic vocals – interspersed with yelps and howls – arresting appearance and no-holds-barred public persona she became something of a celebrity. By the 1980s, after two successful Nina Hagen Band albums, she began working as a solo act, and her international reputation grew as her musical styles diversified – ranging from a cover of Rita Pavone's hit 'If I Were a Boy' with a feminist twist to performing the works of Brecht/Weill with a full orchestra and Bizet's *Carmen*. In 1990 she announced that she believed in UFOs and publicly espoused some esoteric views but later embraced Christianity. In 1998 she released a version of the Union Berlin fans' chant 'Eisern Union', which has the honour of being German football's top rock anthem. Hagen's most celebrated single, 'Smack Jack', from her first solo album *NunSexMonkRock*, was ubiquitous in Germany in 1982 – and also enjoyed some success in other European countries (it reached number 7 in Norway). Composed by Ferdinand Karmelk, her partner at the time, it dealt with the desperation of heroin addiction. Ever eccentric, non-conformist and never dull, in addition to her career in music she has, among other things, been an actress, TV presenter and launched a range of underwear – truly a unique and multi-faceted talent.

BFC Dynamo, meanwhile, has the usual problems that come with playing in a regional league: not enough money, too few sponsors, overburdened volunteers and fixtures that attract little attention.

Then there's the issue of some of the personalities at the club, such as strongman financier Peter Meyer, a former hooligan, or Rainer Lüdtke, the club's long-standing head of supporter relations. Lüdtke once told Berlin's *Tageszeitung* that the war flag of the German Reich had been desecrated by the Nazis, and he once said he could see no reason to take exception to the idea of a day for the German people – not the kind of utterances likely to attract sponsors to the club, but the message seems to get through to BFC Dynamo supporters.

'We have done a great deal to move away from the image we had at that time,' says Lüdtke. 'Like other clubs we have players from different nations, especially in our youth teams. There we have a high proportion of young players with a migrant background. We've had a Turkish coach. I think it's a shame that such details go unnoticed and that we as a club should have to point them out. But we don't have the funds to start big image campaigns.' These are the kinds of words one is used to hearing from those who deflect accusations of racism, and such statements explain how right-wing structures can exist comfortably alongside migrant workers, especially in football. Lüdtke portrays the BFC of today as a victim of the media, while speaking of 'radicalism' instead of right-wing extremism when discussing the 1990s. Still, there is genuine progress – in combatting violence in particular and in the work with fans – and problematic links are said to have been severed. Evidently such developments do not receive much public attention.

What then does East Germany mean for BFC? The club's fan base, as many describe it, has, unlike that of Union, hardly changed. It's dominated by older men from the East for whom BFC Dynamo has always provided a natural home. There are still right-wing forces among them, but these are perhaps easier to spot in a relatively small supporter base. BFC has spent the past few years trying to attract more people to its new home in the currently hip district of Prenzlauer Berg, without much success so far, whereas the hipster image seems to come naturally to Union.

Perhaps match days at the BFC ground still feel stuck in a communist-era time capsule, with GDR flags in the crowd and chants coming from some BFC supporters about the FDGB-Pokal (the old East German Cup) and the old GDR greeting '*Sport frei!*' ('Free sport!') – however ironically these are delivered – and there is also perhaps an added sense of longing for the past or a wish to be provocative. Of course, the club also lacks the money and success needed to create a spirit of optimism.

'We certainly still have an East German identity, but it doesn't play that great a role,' says Lüdtke. 'We traditionally saw ourselves as a club from the East, but today we are one Germany.'

The contrast with Union's sense of its identity is palpable. Then again, Lüdtke does not have half of Europe as potential supporters, just Berlin. He does have a youth team with young players coming up for whom the East–West divide means nothing. The old identity can be left behind, but the economic gaps remain. At the time of writing there is just one club from the former GDR in the Bundesliga, and it sees its eastern background as only a part of its history as a Berlin club. ✒

The Island of Youth

Pedalo traffic around the Insel der Jugend, the Island of Youth, Treptower Park. In the background are the chimneys of the Rummelsburg industrial zone.

You don't have to leave the city to escape from it;
just head for one of Berlin's many green lungs. The
Island of Youth, as it became known during the GDR
years, is one of these oases, somewhere you can
forget that the city lies just across the water.

JÖRG SUNDERMEIER
Translated by Claudio Cambon

I was the GDR. And I was a lot of things before that. I was Brandenburg, Prussia, the first German Reich. I was democracy and the Third Reich. I was the Occupied Zone and, yes, the GDR. Well, that's not entirely true. Half of me was GDR, but the other half was freedom, the 'independent political unit', as the East called it. I was two capitals, one without a function and with limited opportunity to travel. I was an island and part of a pact. I was a special zone, and I was special. I was always a capital, and now I am a capital once again. I am Berlin.

I have always been a green city, at first a joining of Berlin and Cölln, followed by other towns and villages. After the Second World War I became even greener. I have always been a border town because I grew over borders. I grew over the border to Charlottenburg and the border to Rixdorf. I swallowed the city of Spandau, which is older than me, and I swallowed other municipalities as well. My hunger is still not sated.

I have always been a green city because of the way that I extended my borders. I expanded into areas at the periphery that had not yet in every case been built upon; these had at the core former villages not by then given over to urban-style housing, where development then stopped in many cases and will not start again – because each of my neighbourhoods has a centre of which it is proud.

I also granted myself the Tiergarten, a zoological garden in the city centre that is bigger than any castle grounds – and I allowed myself some castle grounds, too. And why just one zoo when you can have two? I have two zoos, one in the West and one in the East.

And the most recent border that I over-ran, the Mauer, the Wall, brought lots of green space with it. Ride your bike along the Mauerweg path and you'll see. In Prenzlauer Berg it even opens out into a park, the Mauerpark.

For some time now I have been even greener, because there were bomb sites everywhere in 1945 that were never redeveloped. Allotments stood where factories had been, playgrounds where there used to be houses and wild green spaces (which later became parks) where once a train station stood. Mounds of rubble, too: the Teufelsberg, the Devil's Mountain, in the western section of Berlin, and in the eastern half, Mont Klamott in Friedrichshain park, a mound that had once been a bunker that was covered over with rubble from the war for which the bunker had been built. We were ashamed of the war, so we hid the bunker.

Then there are cemeteries, green spaces also, only they are not used so much for burials any longer. People now prefer to be cremated rather than have flamboyant graves erected after their deaths, but in the late 19th century there was no end to the

JÖRG SUNDERMEIER is a journalist and director of the award-winning Berlin publishing house Verbrecher Verlag, which he co-founded in 1995. He is the author and editor of several volumes on the city of Berlin, including a book on Sonnenallee, a famous street in the Neukölln district, and a 2017 guide to the city's most evocative cemeteries, *11 Berliner Friedhöfe, die man gesehen haben muss, bevor man stirbt* ('11 Berlin Cemeteries That You Should See Before You Die').

marble and granite that people wanted to pile on top of their graves. After the war the Wall suddenly cut these cemeteries off from their parishes, and consequently people started to use them more as parks. Now they are places where, while people aren't giving concerts as such, you can read or eat in cafés that have been opened in buildings in the former cemetery grounds. Someone's corpse may still lie buried just a few metres from your table. A long-unused cemetery in Neukölln was deconsecrated and redesignated as a public park, the Anita-Berber-Park, named after the erotic dancer and actress who died in 1928 at just twenty-nine years of age and whose remains are still interred there. People come here at the weekend to have a beer above abandoned graves, which the darkly inclined dancer would surely have appreciated.

This is who I am. These are my green spaces. This is the present. But where is the future?

When half of me was still the capital of the GDR everything was about the future. I had significant problems at the time, pressing production issues, loyalty issues – and procurement didn't always work as smoothly as it should. But those were all macro-problems, the kind of state problems that affect a capital but aren't its personal issues; ones that a city cannot fix by itself.

In my eastern zone I definitely had plenty of smaller problems, too, city problems. The questions were: how do I set up a park, and what do I do with an island?

A state doesn't just have people and machines to organise. A state must also deal with the legacy of the states that preceded it, things like bunkers and ideologies. How do you get the wrong state out of your mind? runs the question that every state must ask itself. A very ambitious GDR also wondered whether to go for a clean break or a smooth transition. The people were liberated from the state that had been, but their freedom had not yet been consolidated. The previous state always had to be understood as the opposite of the GDR, as was the west of the country.

As a capital city my east did its best to contribute to the GDR's self-determination; my west countered socialism with consumerism, its huge advertisements beaming eastwards – I really was quite schizophrenic back then. How then – this was the question – were we to find a way around the actual present, with all its historical baggage, into the kind of present in which the future might emerge?

It began with experimentation. There was Treptower Park, a large, 88-hectare space that was opened in 1888 after twelve years of construction. Parts of it were ripped up again in 1896 to make a way for the Great Industrial Exposition of Berlin, which was situated around an artificial lake. The exhibition was laid out like a *Gesamtkunstwerk*: an Alpine panorama, a pyramid and a theatre were built, even its own underground railway, the Knüppelbahn, which ran trains through the tunnel under the Spree until 1932 and continued to operate as a pedestrian underpass for several more years. It had its own station, which, like the entire exhibition, was closed again, according to plan, in October 1896 after just six months. By that time many tonnes of bratwurst and cake had been consumed, and the beer (there were roughly a dozen

A picnic on a jetty on the Island of Youth.

outlets) flowed freely. People marvelled at the record output of German industry – but the most important thing was that Berliners, intent on enjoying themselves, were given six months of something they wanted, and it attracted around seven million visitors. Today hardly any traces of the buildings and facilities erected for the fair remain; almost everything was torn down shortly after it closed.

And then the park had a few years of peace and quiet. Today the Soviet Memorial stands where the heart of the trade fair once was. It commemorates the sacrifices made by the Soviet Union in the war started by the Germans. Many statues were erected in the park under the GDR, but the basic layout didn't change. Peace and quiet was important for anyone living in the city, even in the GDR.

Treptower Park impresses with its size. Unlike the Viktoriapark in Kreuzberg, opened as a recreation area at roughly the same time, Treptower cannot be so readily grasped. Its breadth lends itself to wandering, and its size demands contemplation.

But there is no rest without relaxation; the Eierhäuschen restaurant, which the realist novelist Theodor Fontane wrote about, has stood next to the park since the 19th century. And, beside that, the Kulturpark Plänterwald, which was opened in 1969 as a prestige project for the GDR, a kind of Tivoli Gardens with a Ferris wheel and everything else you could possibly wish for. Tonnes of bratwurst and cake were consumed here, too, and the beer flowed freely. After the Wall came down, the park was renamed the Spreepark, but it flopped spectacularly, and it closed (see the sidebar on page 172). Plans for its reopening have so far come to nothing. Next to the park the Gasthaus Zenner, which opened in 1822 as a municipal coffee house and has been added to and rebuilt several times, also offers entertainment in the form of bratwurst, cake and beer. Up to 1,500 people can have a Sunday drink here, and hundreds do exactly that every weekend in summer.

Looking across the river from the Spreepark or from the *Biergarten* of the Gasthaus Zenner, you can see the Insel der Jugend, the Island of Youth.

Up to the mid-19th century this island in the middle of the Spree was isolated and overgrown, welcoming only the occasional fisherman or perhaps a couple of lovebirds who might row over to it. The island passed into private ownership and was enlarged with waste material and sand. Rabbits were bred there. While the Great Industrial Exposition of Berlin was running it was integrated into the fair as the island known as Neu-Spreeland (New Spreeland) on which the 'ruins' of an 'abbey' were constructed; these burned down in 1914. A beautiful and dramatic steel truss bridge leads over to the newly erected buildings on the island. These still evoke another time: the gatehouse, home now to the club Insel, resembles a tower. Incidentally, in the way that fiction often becomes reality, the bridge is called the Abteibrücke, the Abbey Bridge, even if no real monastic community ever actually stood there. Behind the gatehouse, on the other side of this narrow island, is a hostel, built shortly after the war, where young girls in need can seek refuge from their parents.

The club became a sensation after the Wall fell. Fabulous events were held. Indie acts shared the stage with DJs, and huge crowds flocked here. In the 1990s people would arrive late into the night, walking through the unlit park, which was often patrolled by skinheads on the lookout for prey.

The cultural activities are a bit sleepier

now, but that's all right, because the island is the island, a safe haven. In the summertime there is a *Biergarten* where you can rent out kayaks and rowing boats. The music is low, the food is good and the beer even better – it's so different from the other side of the bridge on the mainland. Even though many people sit in the *Biergarten*, it's less hearty, less folksy, less *Berlin*. (I should say at this point that what is often put about as being my particular 'character' or that of my inhabitants doesn't really exist; it's a cliché – worse, as with all clichés, there are now many people who want to live that cliché.)

So much for the *Biergarten*. It stands between the club and the hostel. And it's out of consideration for those who live nearby that the behaviour one will encounter here is polite, courteous and well behaved.

The *Biergarten*, hostel and club take up only around half the island. The rest is untouched by commerce: if you want to eat, you bring your own food. This is where you will find students spending time during their vacations, smoking and drinking, meeting or making friends from all over the world. Phones play music, people sing and strum the guitar, but, importantly, not too loudly; they don't want to bother the little group sitting next door – and, hey, the hostel is right there, too.

They sit there on one part of me and look around. From the *Biergarten* they can see the Eierhäuschen covered in scaffolding and the closed-down amusement park. From the green area of the island they look, albeit briefly, towards the Zenner restaurant and Treptower Park and then out over the Spree or towards Stralau and its peninsula. Stralau and Treptow once fiercely contested ownership of this small island until it was given to Neukölln. That was before 1920 when I annexed all three

COMMUNITY GARDENS

Schrebergärten, community gardens, are a true passion for Germans, Berliners especially. Citizens rent these small allotments, which are often publicly owned, to grow their own food and give them the sense of having their own garden, even if it isn't right outside their front door. *Schrebergärten* first appeared in the 19th century, during the period of full industrialisation, as a social measure for the new urban proletariat. Originally, in addition to giving workers the opportunity to grow more nourishing, vitamin-rich food, the gardens were also intended to be play spaces for children. For many years they were viewed as the quintessential attribute of the German bourgeoisie, but the growth of urban gardening has led to their reappraisal. As a place to escape the frenetic pace of the city, their allure has never dimmed.

Community gardens in Germany

Berlin	67,961
Hamburg	35,641
Leipzig	32,000
Dresden	23,500
Bremen	16,633
Frankfurt	15,870
Cologne	13,000

Members of community garden associations

Germany	970,000
Poland	850,000
Slovakia	130,000
UK	80,000
Belgium	42,000
Denmark	40,000
Austria	38,000

SOURCE: WIKIPEDIA

of those formerly independent municipalities – the island, too. But these three places seldom hold their gaze.

Their attention is instead directed towards something they could never see with the ruins of the amusement park right behind them or the GDR-era art just in front of them or from within the grounds of the Soviet Memorial. It's something they could not see from the mainland, something that opens itself to the eye only when the space allows – something that they see because they are on the Island of Youth.

The island is a special place, and whoever it was in the city administration of my eastern part who came up with the idea that we should stop calling it Rohr-Insel, Treppbruch, Neu-Spreeland or Abteiinsel and instead give it the name Insel der Jugend got it just right. Not because of the girls' hostel, not because of the rowers or the young couples who come to drink a Berliner Weisse and stuff their kids with fries – no, not because of them. Whoever it was, they got the name just right because the island has an effect on everyone who comes here just to hang out. And the right to hang out is a privilege afforded to the young.

They don't often look at the Zenner in the Spreepark or at the Stralau peninsula with its ghastly newbuilds. The kids take over the island and listen to music, talk, smoke dope, drink, fool around, snooze and look up at the sky beyond the clouds to see what's coming. They look to the future because they are the future. My future. They see the Berlin that hasn't yet come to be but is just up ahead. They look out from an earlier part of the natural world, from a piece of Prussia. They walk along the walls that stood through the Nazi era and the GDR, the fall of the Wall and the onset of capitalism. Sitting or lying on this green island they see a better Berlin in their future. They see me. 🦅

The first amusement park in the GDR – the Kulturpark Plänterwald – was inaugurated in 1969, close to the Island of Youth. Shrouded in greenery and characterised by its classic panoramic Ferris wheel, this attraction was wildly popular, drawing huge numbers of visitors every year. It was privatised after German reunification, the concession awarded to the amusement park operator Norbert Witte, despite his less than immaculate track record. (In 1981 there was an accident on one of his rides in the Hamburg amusement park that left seven people dead.) Born into the trade – his father Otto was a park operator, who went down in history for claiming to have been crowned King of Albania in 1913 by exploiting his resemblance to Prince Halim ed-Din – he inherited his father's unorthodox business approach and his megalomania. Despite a drop in the number of visitors year on year, he continued to expand the park, renaming it the Spreepark, until 2001 when he filed for bankruptcy. Witte loaded up some of his rides into twenty shipping containers and fled to Peru, where he tried to start again by winning over a public not used to modern amusement parks; however, his roller coasters continued to nosedive, and this great adventure ended up dead in the water, too, stymied by local bureaucracy and corruption. He tried to climb out of this hole by shipping one of his rides, the Flying Carpet, back to Germany packed with 180 kilos of cocaine, but the Peruvian police rumbled him. The Spreepark has remained abandoned since 2002; vegetation grows through the rusted rides – and on very windy days the Ferris wheel turns all by itself, carrying its own ghosts.

Last Orders

Even before the Covid-19 pandemic, Berlin's *Eckkneipen* – traditional pubs that could be found on many a street corner – were in crisis. They were once meeting places where all social classes mixed, an extension of people's living rooms, but times have changed.

FABIAN FEDERL
Translated by Claudio Cambon

Left: A customer at
Zur Molle, an *Eckkneipe*
in the Neukölln district.

My grandmother used to run a bistro in the east of France, in a small mining town south of Lyon. For much of the day there would be a handful of customers, either those left over from breakfast or those who were there for an aperitif, depending on the time of day. Some would play table football in the back room, while others sat at the bar drinking coffee or wine, perhaps listening to one of the local politicians who would keep office hours at the bistro. At five o'clock, when the shift ended at the mine, the place would fill up. Long after the mine had closed down, five o'clock was still peak rush hour. The bistro was the social centre of this small town, a place for fellowship, socialising, news, free time and celebrations.

Later, when I lived for a short while in Paris, my days were structured by bistros. I ate breakfast in a bistro, spent my evenings in one reading a book and met colleagues and friends there. I often went to a bistro to write. Whenever I entered a bistro, I instantly felt I belonged.

In his work *Éloge du bistrot parisien* ('In Praise of the Parisian Bistro'; Payot, 2015) the anthropologist Marc Augé described the bistro as 'the site of the mingling of the species, of tragedy and comedy, of the words that say nothing and the silences that speak volumes, of loud laughter, stifled moans and a diffuse melancholy'.

The 85-year-old recalls the times he spent with Jean-Paul Sartre in the bistros of the Latin Quarter. He recounts the evenings he whiled away in them as a student talking with professors and later, as a professor himself, with students. He describes the waitress in the bistro below his apartment, dissecting the dance around the bar, the 'nerve centre', which, as Augé says, belonged to no one but which offered everyone a seat. You don't have to go into a bistro to know 'the bistro', he writes. It is a kind of intangible cultural locus that clearly evokes certain ideas, even outside France.

Since I moved to Berlin I have often asked myself whether such a place exists here. And if so, where? A place for the young and the old, early and late, above and below. I have ordered books and illustrated volumes published in the last three decades about Berlin's food-service industry, and especially about the Berlin *Eckkneipe*, the corner pub, because that's where I suspected I would find it. The first thing I learned is that the corner pub doesn't have to be on a corner; the second was that maybe it wasn't what I was looking for after all.

THE KNEIPE OFTEN OPENS A WINDOW INTO THE STAIRWELL FOR VENTILATION

The *Kneipe* was originally a place for students to meet and drink. Since the 18th

FABIAN FEDERL is a freelance journalist originally from France who lives and works between Berlin, Lisbon and Rio de Janeiro. He writes for the newspapers *Süddeutsche Zeitung* and *Der Tagesspiegel* as well as the weekly magazine *Die Zeit*. His investigations have been published by titles such as *Elle*, *Brand Eins*, *Reportagen*, *Internazionale* and *Libération*.

century the word has been used to describe a place that serves beer, and later wine, for places with or without a kitchen, big or small. In 1831 C.B. von Ragotzky wrote in his student dictionary *Der flotte Bursch* ('The Lively Lad') that '*Kneipe* generally refers to any public house.' What these varied places all shared was their purpose: *knipen* in Middle High German means something along the lines of 'being close together'.

Der Spiegel magazine wrote in 1975 that 'people in public houses do not live on beer alone', and a study by the Gesellschaft für Marktforschung (Market Research Association) revealed that people went to public houses 'for social reasons' almost 70 per cent of the time, especially 'because I want a change of scene', 'to meet friends and acquaintances' and, last but not least, 'because that's where I have my regular table'. A public living room where all are equal before the landlord.

On the ground floor of the building where I live in Berlin there's an *Eckkneipe*. If I lie on the floor of my bedroom with my ear to the boards I can easily eavesdrop on conversations. Wednesdays has live music, and I can hear the *Kneipe*, whether I want to or not. The *Kneipe* often opens a window into the stairwell for ventilation, and then I can smell it, too. And often, when on my way out in the morning and I step on broken glass, I curse it.

I rarely go in, and, when I do, I usually don't stay for long. One day I did go in early and leave late, though ... long enough to witness the changeover from the day shift (those who had been here for many hours) to the night crew.

THE SHIFT CHANGEOVER BEGAN AT 9 P.M.
To my right at the bar sat a man in his late forties with light-coloured hair wearing a beige jacket. In front of him was a spiral notepad, a newspaper and a pocket calculator. He entered figures into the device, murmured, tapped, noted and muttered 'OK'. Every now and then he took a sip from his water glass. To my left sat some older men with half-drunk beers. One of them would periodically press his lips together, mumble something and nod a lot. Another rested on his arms clasped over his round belly. Behind them were a few men with bald spots and women with perms and dark rings under their eyes. Time after time a wave of throaty, rattling laughter would course through the room, and, when the laughter subsided, the coughing would begin.

Whenever the heavy brown door slammed shut, it would go quiet for a few moments as the people in the room surveyed the new arrivals and vice versa. And then everyone went back to doing their own thing.

The shift changeover began at 9 p.m. The door opened at more frequent intervals. The men entering the room became younger and stood taller; the men who left were old. When young women walked through the door, the older men sat up straighter on their barstools and adjusted their shirt collars. When young men with stylish haircuts walked in, the older generation sneered a little and went back to their drinks.

Service shifted from one end of the bar to the other as the older people drank less and less. And when an older person gave up their stool, younger people laid their jackets on it and stood around it. The room became louder, more crowded – stifling. And livelier.

I left shortly after midnight. The oldest person in the room by that point was the woman in her late thirties behind the bar.

Perhaps I seldom go into the *Kneipe* in my building because it is too close. But I

Above: A customer at Zur Molle.
Below: Zur Molle's landlord and landlady, Jens and Melanie.

Above: A bottle of Berliner Kindl on the bar of Zur Molle.
Below: Landlord Jens gives his mother a kiss.

Last Orders

do regularly go to other places like it, to *Kneipen* that have this same structure of wooden counters, wall decorations depicting hills somewhere in Germany with roaring stags and wagon wheels, enamelled placards of historical advertisements for beer that is 'fresh and aromatic' or 'substantial and wholesome', hand-carved beer mugs resting on the bar's wooden panelling, humorous slogans like 'Hops and malt are good for the rut', the old gentlemen and waiting staff with their hair dyed blonde.

Is this Berlin's equivalent of the place of fellowship that Augé finds in the Parisian bistro? Whichever way, as an umbrella term for a place that everyone knows, a *Kneipe* seems as good as a bistro.

BARELY FOUND, ALREADY THREATENED
Also, thinking of how all of life can be seen in one place and a single place can take centre stage in your life, the *Kneipe*, according to its apologists, seems comparable to the bistro. The *Eckkneipe* is characterised by 'solitude and socialising, belonging and not belonging and calm and restlessness', according to the writer Clemens Füsers. In his book *Berliner Jahrhundertkneipen* ('Century-old *Kneipen* in Berlin'; Lehmstedt-Verlag, 2011), Füsers, together with the photographer Gudrun Olthoff, visited some of Berlin's oldest *Kneipen*, including the Diener Tattersall in Charlottenburg, the Alte Kolkschenke in Spandau and the Leydicke in Schöneberg. In another work, *Letzte Runde?* ('Last Orders?'; Wasmuth & Zohlen, 2009), they compiled a 'municipal historical inventory' of Berlin's traditional *Eckkneipen*. Given that they are so concerned with heritage, understandably they drew attention to its destruction. This occurred more frequently in areas where the city was undergoing rapid transformation. Füsers wrote that

during his research he found just one old *Eckkneipe* in the Mitte neighbourhood and only two or three in Prenzlauer Berg.

A hundred and fifty years ago Berlin had the highest density of public houses of any city in Europe. The 1806 Berlin Lexicon recorded 155,000 inhabitants and seven hundred inn-keepers (running food businesses whose revenues came mostly from their bars), which meant 221 inhabitants per establishment. In 1905 there were just 157 inhabitants per establishment. According to the catalogue for an exhibition about Berlin's *Kneipen*, there were 364 inhabitants per establishment in 1980, and the visitBerlin site states there are currently about nine hundred traditional *Kneipen* for 3.77 million Berliners, which means just one for every four thousand inhabitants. The downward trend is irrefutable: according to Germany's hotel-industry associations, since 2008 the number of *Kneipen* in Germany has fallen from 38,549 to 31,650; a drop of 18 per cent; 6,899 dead *Kneipen*.

Big cities in many countries have for some time acknowledged the disappearance of their pubs and bars as a cultural phenomenon, as has the literature that deals with the subject. In Germany the media publish obituaries, the Wikipedia entry for *Kneipe* has a whole section on the subject and local breweries vie with one another in their strategies to save these institutions. For example, in Berlin the Schultheiss brewery publishes a guide to neighbourhood *Kneipen*, organises the All-Night Neighbourhood *Kneipe* Festival, selects the 'best neighbourhood *Kneipe*' and escorts German singer and actor Frank Zander around the city on a horse-drawn brewer's dray.

Any number of illustrated books, guidebooks and even novels have been published that chart the decline of the *Kneipe*, and

> 'Big cities in many countries have for some time acknowledged the disappearance of their pubs and bars as a cultural phenomenon, as has the literature that deals with the subject.'

they all convey the same message: let's give them one last hurrah before they disappear completely! And why should this be of interest? *Kneipen* can no longer draw in the customers – or not enough of them – to pay the rent, so they are forced to close. That's how it works in other areas. People just go elsewhere or they drink at home or – better yet – not at all.

All the literature makes it clear that a *Kneipe* is more than just a pub, by emphasising its social function: the idea of 'being close together' in the word's original meaning, to people searching for a place for 'social reasons', as *Der Spiegel* noted, to notions associated with the sense of 'belonging and not belonging', as Füsers has written. A place where society's members can meet casually or by chance. An *agora* with beer. What the sociologist Ray Oldenburg calls a 'third place' and which, as such, can be compared with the bistro as Augé describes it and as I experienced it: a place that stands between one's home and workplace. A meeting place, like a park, café, library, museum, church or bookshop. Oldenburg characterises this space as beneficial or free. It does not draw any distinctions based on status or capital; it sets no conditions, is open to all and makes no demands. The third place is essentially open to everyone in society. It is a place of contact. It's not necessarily a place in which friendships are formed; it's more like the metro, where people stand next to one another wearing earbuds. Oldenburg writes that it is essential to

the workings of a democracy because it provides a public space where below and above, left and right, outer and inner all mingle. And through encounters and contact with others it reminds us that none of us is the norm, whether we're rich or poor, a secondary-school teacher or a foreman, a regular or someone who's just wandered in. The hardening towards people who live or think differently that we find in online filter bubbles and echo chambers can be ironed out here. Every city and every country has their own version of this; think of the Vienna coffee house (recognised by UNESCO as having 'intangible cultural heritage') or the British pub or free house, which expresses its function in its very name.

WHY SHOULD WE MOURN THE KNEIPE?

The question is simply, does the Berlin *Kneipe* still embody the ideals of the third place? Before me lies an exhibition catalogue that hails the *Kneipe* as the 'place where members of political parties meet, the favourite hangout of sport clubs, social clubs, provident societies, a place for big family gatherings, a refuge for the solitary and the lonely, an oasis for the thirsty and a regular meeting point for the petit bourgeoisie and army and navy veterans' groups'. But the catalogue in which these words – by former Berlin housing minister Peter Ulrich – appear dates back to 1980, a year in which *Der Spiegel* proclaimed that 'People are drinking more than ever before … It appears that the German *Kneipe* has withstood the test of time, competition from television and beer in a bottle, the weight-loss movement, Coca-Cola ideology and legislation on maximum blood-alcohol levels.'

In Berlin and other major cities internationally a certain glamour factor has contributed to the celebration of the everyman's pub. Media personalities drag the *Eckkneipe* into the tabloid press and so into the hands of women at the hairdresser's and of men in – yes, you guessed it – *Kneipen*. One well-known German actress, Brigitte Mira, who was famous for her portrayals of an everywoman and who was associated in the German national consciousness with *Kneipen* culture, once wrote: 'What is so seductive about the Berlin *Eckkneipe* is that you can approach it from two directions.' Although she meant this in a spatial sense – i.e. the two roads that lead to the corner at which it is situated – we can also read it as a description of the *Kneipe* as a social space: it is the midpoint where people from every rung of the social ladder come together.

The connection between a watering hole and culture, high or popular, didn't start with Mira. Max Stirner's Radical Doctor's Club used to meet in the red salon of the Café Stehely on the Jägerstrasse. Regularly in attendance was a young Karl Marx. Earlier, in the late 18th century, Heinrich Heine and Joseph von Eichendorff used to meet at the Café Josty on the Joachimsthaler Strasse, and, a hundred years later, Theodor Fontane and Adolph Menzel also went there to argue over who the most important German realist was. And even if such establishments hardly qualified as simple beer parlours, they were nevertheless pioneers in the spread of literacy and politicisation of the masses. Today *Kneipen* remain perfect venues for public debate, for wider-ranging dialogues outside official control. Anyone present is free to speak their mind.

But who is still there?

KNEIPE CUSTOMERS TODAY ARE ACTUALLY PEOPLE SEEKING OUT HIP PUBS

The *Kneipe* on the ground floor of my building, in a former working-class neighbourhood of West Berlin, has been there since the early 1970s. In the building there are doctors' surgeries, shared flats, young families and a few long-term residents. Above, on the fourth floor, the majestic figure of an angel rises over a large late-19th-century balcony. The apartment block has been repaired but not refurbished; as a result, it probably still expresses some of the typical diversity that was once the goal of urban planning here.

'In the apartment block, children come out of the basement residences to go to the free school using the same hallway as the children of the teacher or the salesman who are on their way to the *Gymnasium* high school,' wrote James Hobrecht, the 19th-century architect and planner who shaped Berlin more than anyone else: a city of apartment blocks in which social mixing was encouraged so that those who were better off could see the needs of the poor first hand and people such as 'civil servants, artists, scholars, teachers, etc.' would prove inspiring models to uneducated families, 'even just by being there and through their silent example', a mixing that could be conducted below, above or at the next street corner in the *Kneipe*.

Today the children of the 'teacher or the salesman' rarely live alongside the children of seamstresses or cleaning ladies in the same house or even on the same block. The segregation in residential neighbourhoods also segregates the potential customers for the local *Kneipe*. In the city centre they also have to contend with the fact that

SPÄTI

The *Späti*, a contraction of *Spätkauf* or *Spätverkaufstelle*, the all-night convenience store, stays open late and sells everything from everyday stuff to fripperies, from toilet paper to Rotkäppchen (a fairly unpretentious sparkling wine from the former GDR), milk, pasta, rice, alcohol, ice cream, detergent, cookies and the like. It's also a café and bar that sells basics such as newspapers and cigarettes and offers postal services. The *Späti* is a unique institution highly prized by night owls and the disorganised, of which the city is full. Some years ago shops were ordered to close on Sundays (although this was put on hold during the Covid-19 lockdowns; they're obviously 'essential'), and, while *Spätis* are supposed to observe this ordinance, they often ignore it, which has given rise to some debate about this iconic and apparently indispensable component of Berlin's identity. They began in the 1970s in the GDR to meet the needs of factory workers on night shifts who had to shop at unusual hours. *Spätis* have become important local reference points, even if they do depend on tourism to get by and the pandemic has threatened the survival of many.

their business model, the sale of standard alcohol at moderate prices, even in the presence of relatively brisk demand, is barely competitive. Bars and boutiques are driving up rents, and this or that landlord hopes for something more prestigious and lower in emissions in their building than a smokers' local. There may well have been reasons other than purely financial that the former owners of the famous *Kneipe* Wilhelm Hoeck in Charlottenburg found themselves in trouble after they sold it to be turned into a pharmacy in 2017, but it is clear that such a landmark pub's closing after 125 years suggests that the long-term survival of the traditional neighbourhood *Kneipe* is anything but secure.

Added to this is the fact that people's going-out habits have changed markedly in recent years. '*Kneipe* customers today are actually people seeking out hip pubs. Unlike in the past, they don't automatically go to their neighbourhood *Kneipe* for every occasion; they instead look for places that match their mood,' wrote trend researcher Peter Wippermann in 2012 in *Die Welt*. When there is no choice, in rural or suburban areas, the *Kneipe* can at times still function as a place for fellowship, but in big cities, where *Eckkneipen* still occupy many street corners, if there's a fashionable, hipster *Kneipe* further down the road from your nearest, the scenes diverge considerably.

Todd Kliman, restaurant critic for *The New Yorker* and *The Washingtonian* described this change in people's going-out habits in the *Oxford American* in 2015. In his essay 'Coding and Decoding Dinner' he describes the tacit cues that explain for whom an establishment is intended. 'A restaurant is a network of codes,' he writes, from the waiter in the tailcoat to service with a low-cut neckline and a tattoo, from the logo of a new, organic

THE HOBRECHT PLAN

As in many 19th-century European cities, Berlin had its own urban development plan. Named after its creator, James Hobrecht, it sought to reorganise the city in a more modern manner. Significant demographic growth had created untenable hygiene conditions, and the arrival of new workers from the countryside prompted the city to reconsider the viability of its residential policies. Hobrecht created an urban development plan based on three fundamental principles: the mixing of the classes, the balance between work and free time and the introduction of the concept of the square. This gave rise to the *Mietskaserne* – the large tenement buildings that today still define the city's urban fabric – in which the various social classes were supposed to meet and mingle. The workers would live on the lower floors, and their richer, better-educated neighbours would live on the upper storeys. The Hobrecht Plan also introduced a new sewer system (until then, effluent still ran along open street gullies) and a new roadmap. This new street layout was developed using a radial system to avoid there being only one centre and to encourage the city to develop several focal points. Despite two world wars and radical, post-war urban development plans in both Berlins, East and the West, the 19th-century imprint on the city remains visible, for example, in its squares and its circular roadway network. Charlottenburg, Reinickendorf, Weissensee, Lichtenberg, Rixdorf and Wilmersdorf were still open countryside then, and the plan included them within the urban area.

beer brand to the Schultheiss sign. Anyone who doesn't fit in is welcome in theory, but they will probably look for a place where they'll feel more of an insider and less of an outsider, making the hip *Kneipe* the logical choice for some. When we look at other places – such as shisha cafés, gay bars and Turkish tearooms – from this perspective, we see how much the notion of the subculture-specific establishment is shaping Berlin. Such spaces enrich the city and make it more interesting, but they do not encourage mixing and equality; they are not 'unconditional' spaces, as per Ray Oldenburg's third spaces, and they are not spaces for the 'mingling of the species', as in Marc Augé's descriptions of bistros.

For the *Eckkneipe*, all these competing places mean the loss of potential customers, which lifestyle changes in society are only exacerbating. Sunday morning is now more about jogging than the morning pint, because health is social capital. Celebrities have become a rarity in the *Eckkneipe*. Smoking? Only outside, if at all. And unions' savings associations or navy veterans' groups either no longer meet in the *Kneipe* or they don't exist any more.

In this way the *Eckkneipe* has itself over the years become a kind of cool place in its own right, one of the reasons why I did not instantly recognise it as a third place when I first came to Berlin. It has its own unstated codes: 'drinkers only', 'fifty and over' or 'no non-smokers' perhaps, or – the further one moves out from the centre of the city – 'Germans only'. And although young Berliners have in recent years started to step into the few remaining *Eckkneipen* in the centre, they haven't become a part of the whole; they remain alien, a group unto themselves, ironic observers. The divide between the old drinkers and this group is too wide, and the shifts, too, are different. Changeover indeed.

A WOMAN STICKS STAMPS ON A HANDFUL OF LETTERS

I spent Christmas away from Berlin. When I returned on 28 December the city was empty and abandoned, as it always is at this time of year. The light was on in the *Kneipe* below my apartment, as it always is. Over the course of the day the regulars came, but fewer people wandered in at night. People were drinking, as always. The gentleman with the pocket calculator was surely sitting alone at the bar, as perhaps were the coughing ladies. Unexpectedly, nothing was happening. The newcomers were at home with their families, and so the people who stayed had room. No shift changeover tonight, for sure.

As I walked by the *Kneipe* in the late afternoon, I saw that a poster had been stuck up advertising the New Year's Eve party. I walked along, turned right and came upon a brightly lit convenience store. The salesperson in the store was blasting out Turkish music, as he always does. A woman was sticking stamps on a handful of letters. A man bought cigarettes and Chantré brandy and an older woman waited in line with a bunch of flowers. Behind her was a suit with earbuds in leafing through the *Handelsblatt* business newspaper. I bought milk, a newspaper and a small beer, and then I sat down on the bench in front of the entrance and smoked a cigarette.

The customers paid one after the other. The salesperson stood in the doorway, lit a cigarette and, pointing to the car parked in front of us, said, 'Cool car, don't you think?' We chatted for a long time, and then I went home, grabbed my things and walked to the bus stop so that I could go a few streets over to meet up with people more like me. Shortly before midnight the light was still on in the *Kneipe* on the ground floor. Five or six people were sitting inside, the people who are always there. ➤

An Author Recommends

A book, a film and an album to understand Berlin, chosen by:

DAVID WAGNER
Translated by Stephen Smithson

David Wagner is an author and connoisseur of Berlin, who writes books and articles about his walks through the city in the spirit of the *flâneur*. Since his debut novel in 2000, *Meine nachtblaue Hose*, he has published, among others, *Spricht das Kind* (2009), *Vier Äpfel* (2009) – which was nominated for the Deutscher Buchpreis, Germany's most prestigious literary award – and *Welche Farbe hat Berlin* (2011). His book *Leben* (2014) won the Leipzig Book Fair Prize and the best foreign novel of the year award 2014 in the People's Republic of China. In 2014 he was visiting professor of literature at the University of Bern. His most recent novel, *Der vergessliche Riese*, was published in 2019.

THE BOOK
**WALKING IN BERLIN:
A FLÂNEUR IN THE CAPITAL**
Franz Hessel
MIT, 2020 (USA) / Scribe, 2018 (UK)

Although describing a Berlin that no longer exists, Franz Hessel's account of his meanderings through the city, *Walking in Berlin: A Flâneur in the Capital*, is my favourite Berlin walking book. Writing in 1929 his tone is already one of retrospection, with nostalgia for the city he misses, the city of his Berlin youth, now built over, lost. The city he roams is the Continent's largest. Having lived for a long time in Paris, he looks at Berlin afresh. Hessel was a good friend of Walter Benjamin (who had a Berlin childhood of his own), and his son was the Buchenwald survivor and author of *Time for Outrage!* (Twelve USA/Quartet UK, 2011) Stéphane Hessel. He lived with his wife Helen and French writer Henri-Pierre Roché (author of the 1952 novel *Jules et Jim*) in a love triangle that appeared on screen in François Truffaut's hugely successful film adaptation – yes, the *flâneur* Franz Hessel was the model for Jim. 'Walking slowly through lively streets is a special pleasure,' he writes. Like many a reader, I've wandered through Berlin with him and seen the city anew. You can still follow his routes today, although much of what you'll see is different from what he describes. Hessel – and this now seems almost uncanny – was able to imagine Kaiser Wilhelm Memorial Church, not at all old at the time, in ruins; his prophetic gift enabled him to recognise the building's value in that state. It took the Second World War, which he did not survive, to turn his premonition into a reality.

THE FILM
PRINZESSINNENBAD
Bettina Blümner
2007

THE ALBUM
SONGS OF L. AND HATE
Christiane Rösinger
2010

The Berlin film of my youth – and as an expression of yearning for the city, probably *the* quintessential Berlin film – is, of course, Wim Wenders' 1987 classic *Wings of Desire* (*Der Himmel über Berlin*). After seeing it for the first time, somewhere in provincial West Germany, I wanted to go to Berlin and live in that city full of bunkers, angels and ruins. After I did move there a few years later I would sit in Hans Scharoun's Berlin State Library waiting for the angels. In vain. *Der Himmel über Berlin* depicts a Berlin that no longer exists, with bomb craters, the wasteland of Potsdamer Platz and the emptiness that once was West Berlin. Unfortunately, as I see it today, this appealing emptiness in the film is marred by an element of kitsch – and I'd like to recommend an antidote in the form of Bettina Blümner's 2007 documentary, *Prinzessinnenbad* ('Pool of Princesses'). It's a film that portrays three very earthly fifteen-year-old girls from Kreuzberg, Berlin. Their names are Klara, Mina and Tanutscha; they live with their mothers (their fathers – respectively German, Italian and Iranian – are conspicuous by their absence) and have been best friends since kindergarten. The director followed the girls for more than a year; we see them in Kreuzberg's Prinzenbad lido, at parties, at home, in the park – and we see how they turn men's heads: three young women, still almost children, who hold on to their cigarettes as if they're trapeze poles they are going to use to vault through the big top of youth as they somersault into adulthood. One line from the film has become a catchphrase in Berlin: '*Ich komm' aus Kreuzberg, du Muschi*' ('I'm from Kreuzberg, you pussy').

Techno was the sound of the city of ruins to which I moved in 1991. The city danced in clubs, on parades, in cellars and old vaults. What is most emblematic of this time and this music is not any specific cut or individual DJ but the mythical clubs where the music was played – the temples of their day – so it is significant that the reinforced door of Tresor, then the most important techno club, went on to become today, almost thirty years after its opening, one of the first exhibits to be transported to the Humboldt Forum in the rebuilt Berlin Palace. Only in Berlin. The door, which once led to a real vault, is on loan from Tresor's founder, Dimitri Hegemann. He was also an early supporter of the band Die Lassie Singers and its successor Britta, both groups formed around the singer, writer and legend Christiane Rösinger, and it is her 2010 solo album *Songs of L. and Hate* that I would like to bring to your attention here – not just because it contains a song with the title 'Berlin' but because Christiane Rösinger succeeds time and again in conjuring up the city in her music. There are the 'saddest people in all of Berlin', who stand around at night in front of the Imbiss International, and there are 'hostel hordes drooling through the streets'. She sings of the city as she remembers it, where rents were once so low that anyone could live as an artist, when 'going out and standing around' could be seen as a vocation. But she sings also of the transformation brought by the digital bohemia, of the precariousness of art, of gentrification, displacement and change in a city that since the war has always lived on money not generated locally. She sings of Berlin.

The Playlist

You can listen to this playlist at:
open.spotify.com/user/iperborea

A playlist to encapsulate contemporary Berlin. If I had to sum the list up in a single word, I would choose 'open', because it embraces the many genres that make up the city's musical landscape and the diversity of its artists' origins. All of them live in Berlin and burst on to the scene here, even though only three are natives. We begin with the piano playing of Federico Albanese, originally from Milan, who became one of the figureheads of the city's modern classical scene. Alice Phoebe Lou, on the other hand, is South African; having started out as a busker in the Mauerpark, thanks to her incredible voice she now fills stadiums all over the world while remaining an entirely independent artist (who can often still be found playing on the street). British outfit the Underground Youth represent Berlin's psych/new wave movement; from small venues they have progressed to huge European tours. In the same ballpark, we find the Soft Moon, a.k.a. Californian musician Luis Vasquez, who has won over the city with his post-punk, darkwave sounds. With the British-Filipino producer DJ Objekt, we begin to stray into experimental electronica, also represented by Spanish artist JASSS. Dengue Dengue Dengue, meanwhile, hail from Peru; they have a permanent residency at YAAM and have inspired an exciting electro-Latin scene in Berlin.

From Hamburg we have DJ Koze, whose track 'XTC' explores the links between drugs and clubbing; Moderat and Marcel Dettmann are Berliners, on the other hand – genuine local institutions, who join forces on this legendary remix – as is Ruede Hagelstein, who in addition to working as a producer and DJ will be known to clubbers as one of the brains behind the legendary Watergate club. Efdemin is a long-time Berliner and one of the icons of Ostgut Ton, the label owned by that temple of techno, Berghain. The playlist ends with another Italian, Lucy, a 'shaman' originally from Palermo, who brilliantly combines ambient and techno and has left his mark on the city's musical history with his label Stroboscopic Artefacts.

ERCOLE GENTILE
Translated by Alan Thawley

1

Federico
Albanese
Mauer Blues
2018

2

The Soft Moon
Burn
2018

3

Ruede
Hagelstein
Shai
2019

4

Alice Phoebe Lou
*Something
Holy*
2019

5

Objekt
35
2018

6

JASSS
Oral Couture
2017

7

Dengue
Dengue
Dengue
Agni
2019

8

DJ Koze
XTC
2015

9

Moderat
(Marcel
Dettmann
remix)
Bad Kingdom
2013

10

The
Underground
Youth
Alice
2017

11

Efdemin
New Atlantis
2019

12

Lucy
Samsara
2016

Digging Deeper

FICTION

Chloe Aridjis
Book of Clouds
Grove, 2009 (USA) / Vintage, 2010 (UK)

Thomas Brussig
Heroes Like Us
Farrar, Straus & Giroux, 1997

Jenny Erpenbeck
Go, Went, Gone
Granta, 2017

Ernst Haffner
Blood Brothers
Other Press, 2015 (USA) / Vintage, 2016 (UK)

Christopher Isherwood
The Berlin Novels
New Directions, 2008 (USA)
/ Vintage, 1999 (UK)

Wladimir Kaminer
Russian Disco
Ebury Press, 2002

Volker Kutscher
Babylon Berlin
Picador, 2018 (USA) / Sandstone, 2016 (UK)

Jason Lutes
Berlin
Drawn & Quarterly, 2018

Terézia Mora
Day In and Out
Harper Perennial, 2013

Cees Nooteboom
All Souls' Day
Pan Macmillan, 2002 (USA)
/ Picador, 2002 (UK)

Heinz Rein
Berlin Finale
Penguin, 2019

Simon Urban
Plan D
Vintage, 2014

Sven Regener
Berlin Blues
Vintage, 2004

Peter Schneider
The Wall Jumper
Penguin, 2005

Anke Stelling
Higher Ground
Scribe, 2021

Stefanie de Velasco
Tiger Milk
Head of Zeus, 2014

NON-FICTION

Felix Denk and Sven von Thülen
*Der Klang der Familie: Berlin,
Techno and the Fall of the Wall*
Books on Demand, 2014

Anke Fesel and Chris Keller
*Berlin Heartbeats: Stories from
the Wild Years, 1990–Present*
Suhrkamp, 2017

Anna Funder
Stasiland: Stories from Behind the Berlin Wall
Harper Perennial, 2011 (USA)
/ Granta, 2011 (UK)

Gideon Lewis-Kraus
*City of Rumor: The Compulsion
to Write About Berlin*
Readux Books, 2013

Iain MacGregor
*Checkpoint Charlie: The Cold War, the Berlin
Wall and the Most Dangerous Place on Earth*
Scribner, 2020 (USA) / Constable, 2020 (UK)

Rory MacLean
Berlin: Portrait of a City Through the Centuries
(USA) / *Berlin: Imagine a City* (UK)
Picador, 2015 (USA) / Weidenfeld
& Nicholson, 2015 (UK)

Alexandra Richie
Faust's Metropolis: A History of Berlin
HarperCollins, 1999

Peter Schneider
Berlin Now: The City After the Wall
(USA) / *Berlin Now: The Rise
of the City and the Fall
of the Wall* (UK)
Farrar, Straus & Giroux, 2014
(USA) / Penguin, 2014 (UK)

Paul Sullivan and Marcel Krueger
*Berlin: A Literary Guide
for Travellers*
I.B. Tauris, 2016

Frederick Taylor
*The Berlin Wall: A World
Divided 1961–1989* (USA) /
*The Berlin Wall: 13 August
1961–9 November 1989* (UK)
Harper Perennial, 2008 (USA)
/ Bloomsbury, 2009 (UK)

David Wagner
Berlin Triptych
Readux, 2014

Barney White-Spunner
Berlin: The Story of a City
Pegasus, 2021 (USA) / Simon
& Schuster, 2020 (UK)

Graphic design and art direction: Tomo Tomo and Pietro Buffa
Photography: Mattia Vacca
Photographic content curated by Prospekt Photographers
Illustrations: Francesca Arena
Infographics and cartography: Pietro Buffa
Managing editor (English-language edition): Simon Smith

Thanks to: Dirk Brauer, Eleonora Di Blasio, Jonas Gabler, Jascha Grewe, Barbara Griffini, Judith Habermas, Hang Hoang, Philipp Kaufmann, Hannes Köhler, Alisa Anh Kotmair, Nora Mercurio, Marta Nuzzo, Katja Petrowskaja, Thibaut de Ruyter, Fabian Saul, Stephen Smithson, Markus Stich, Jörg Sundermeier, Alice Traverso, Andrea Vogel, David Wagner, Sascha Wölck

The opinions expressed in this publication are those of the authors and do not purport to reflect the views and opinions of the publishers.

http://europaeditions.com/thepassenger
http://europaeditions.co.uk/thepassenger
#ThePassengerMag

The Passenger – Berlin
© Iperborea S.r.l., Milan, and Europa Editions, 2021

Translators: Dutch – Laura Watkinson (Berlin Suite); French – Tina Kover (High Infidelity); German – Claudio Cambon (In the Belly of the Whale, The Island of Youth, Last Orders), Eric Rosencrantz (We Were Like Brothers), Sophie Schlondorff (The Greatest Show in Town), Stephen Smithson (Der Himmel Unter Berlin, The Evicted Generation, East vs. East, Dress Code, An Author Recommends); Italian – Claudio Cambon (sidebars), Jennifer Higgins (editorial, 1990s Clubs, standfirsts), Alan Thawley (Four Square Kilometres of Pure Potential, sidebars, photographer's biography, picture captions, The Playlist, A Sign of the Times)
All translations © Iperborea S.r.l., Milan, and Europa Editions, 2021, except 'Berlin Suite' © Laura Watkinson, 2012, 'We Were Like Brothers', Eric Rosencrantz, 2018, 'The Greatest Show in Town' © Sophie Schlondorff, 2014

ISBN 9781787702820

Printed on Munken Pure thanks to the support of Arctic Paper
Printed by ELCOGRAF S.p.A., Verona, Italy